Flexible Grouping for Literacy in the Elementary Grades

Related Titles of Interest

Supervision of Literacy Programs: Teachers as Grass-Roots Change Agents
Lawrence G. Erickson
ISBN: 0-205-16240-1

Integrated Language Arts: Controversy to Consensus
Lesley Mandel Morrow, Jeffrey K. Smith, and Louise Cherry Wilkinson
ISBN: 0-205-14735-6 paper   ISBN: 0-205-14736-4 cloth

A Handbook for the K–12 Reading Resource Specialist
Marguerite C. Radencich, Penny G. Beers, and Jeanne Shay Schumm
ISBN: 0-205-14081-5

A Green Dinosaur Day: A Guide for Developing Thematic Units in Literature-Based Instruction, K–6
Patricia L. Roberts
ISBN: 0-205-14007-6

Language and Literacy Learning in Multicultural Classrooms
Leslie W. Crawford
ISBN: 0-205-13922-1

Strategies for Guiding Content Reading, Second Edition
Sharon J. Crawley and Lee Mountain
ISBN: 0-205-14886-7

Administration and Supervision of the Reading/Writing Program
Marguerite C. Radencich
ISBN: 0-205-15217-1

▶ Flexible Grouping for Literacy in the Elementary Grades

Marguerite C. Radencich
Dade County Public Schools, Miami, Florida

Lyn J. McKay
Pinellas County Schools, Clearwater, Florida

Allyn and Bacon
Boston • London • Toronto • Sydney • Tokyo • Singapore

For Gene, Dayna, Cathy, Diane, and Beto
M.C.R.

For Malcolm, Steven, Janet, Stacey, and Dad
L.J.M.

Library of Congress Cataloging-in-Publication Data

Radencich, Marguerite C.
  Flexible grouping for literacy in the elementary grades /
Marguerite C. Radencich, Lyn J. McKay.
    p.   cm.
  Includes bibliographical references and index.
  ISBN 0-205-16226-6 (PB)   ISBN 0-205-17497-3 (CB)
  1. Group work in education.   2. Reading (Elementary)   3. Language
arts (Elementary)   4. Literacy.   I. McKay, Lyn J.   II. Title.
LB1032.M26   1995
371.3´95—dc20   94-23629
                                                                        CIP

Printed in the United States of America
10 9 8 7 6 5 4 3 2 1   99 98 97 96 95

▶ Contents

Foreword   *vi*
     Dr. John J. Pikulski, University of Delaware

Preface   *xi*

Acknowledgments   *xii*

About the Authors and Contributors   *xiii*

1   **What Research Says about Grouping in the Past and Present and What It Suggests about the Future**   **1**
     by Rebecca Barr

2   **Keeping Flexible Groups Flexible: Grouping Options**   **25**
     by Marguerite C. Radencich, Lyn J. McKay, and Jeanne R. Paratore

3   **Implementing Flexible Grouping with a Common Reading Selection**   **42**
     by Marguerite C. Radencich, Lyn J. McKay, Jeanne R. Paratore, Gloria L. Plaza, Kay E. Lustgarten, Pat Nelms, and Pamela T. Moore

4   **Literature Circles for the Teaching of Literature-Based Reading**   **66**
     by Wendy C. Kasten

5   **Preparing for and Reacting to Change in Grouping Arrangements**   **82**
     by Marguerite C. Radencich and Lyn J. McKay

6   **Connecting Assessment and Instruction in the Flexibly-Grouped Classroom**   **113**
     by Jeanne R. Paratore

7   **At-Risk Children Can Learn to Read and Write**   **134**
     by Patricia M. Cunningham

8   **Multiple Literacy Contexts in Classrooms: Frameworks, Functions, and Forecasts**   **149**
     by Elfrieda H. Hiebert

Glossary of Strategies   *171*

Index   *173*

Foreword
John I. Pikulski

I recently saw a bumper sticker that read: "Life sure was simpler in the days of Dick and Jane." My first reaction, probably because traffic was moving very slowly, was *"It Sure Was!"* But as I stared at the message in the crawling traffic, I found it increasingly provocative. I wondered if it was a comment on life in general or whether this was the car of a teacher expressing her frustration with what seem to be endless "innovations" in education. As I recall, Dick and Jane were at their height of popularity as basal reader characters in the early 1950s, the decade preceding the social turmoil of the 1960s, which changed our culture and lives forever. In the 1950s there was, for example, less concern about poverty and less awareness of cultural and ethnic diversity. The problems and issues were all there, but there was less willingness to admit their existence, let alone attempt to address them. Life was simpler, but given the widespread denial of problems and failure to respect human differences, I'm not at all sure it was better—and in many ways it was worse.

I was in my primary grade years in the 1950s in a small school in northeastern Pennsylvania, so I don't know what it was like to be a teacher then, but based on my own memories and on what I've read, I think that life in schools was simpler then. I know that, at least in my school, organizing for instruction, especially reading instruction, was simpler. All of us in our primary grade classes had a copy of the same Dick-and-Jane-like basal (actually, mine was about Mac and Muff, a cat and dog), and we all took turns reading aloud from it. Then we answered questions and filled in page after page of our workbooks.

Organizing for instruction (or lack of it) sure was simple, but it wasn't very good. I still remember (honestly) how extraordinarily boring reading was. I don't think I was a great reader, but I remember, specifically in third grade, finishing the entire basal in the first month of school. Like many of my classmates, I silently read ahead while other classmates slowly read paragraphs aloud to the whole class. When I had finished the basal, I realized there would be nothing new to read for the rest of the school year; we had neither a classroom library nor even a school library.

Simple, maybe, but not very good! In addition to being boring, reading was often painful. It was painful for the poor readers (yes, there were poor readers even in the days of Dick and Jane), who struggled to read aloud and were embarrassed in front of the whole class by their failures. Organization for instruction was simple; it was also terrible!

Probably because of the difficulties I've outlined, and many others that space limitations prevent me from mentioning, there was a widespread shift away from whole class, round-robin oral reading to delivering reading instruction to groups of children. Group membership was based on reading proficiency, and students in any given group read from a basal that was "at their reading level." Most teachers settled into having three reading groups, one at grade level, one above, and one below. Organization for instruction was not as simple as in the days of Dick and Jane, but it still was pretty simple.

Grouping students into three ability groups prevailed until very recently, but ability grouping for reading instruction had its problems, too (see Chapter 1 of this book). The accumulating evidence suggested, convincingly, that students assigned to the low group, who tended to remain in that group year after year, were particularly penalized by this organizational structure.

Particularly for the past three to five years, classroom teachers who are using basal or basal-like programs have been urged (in many cases required) to abandon their three ability groups and replace them with flexible groups. Along with using flexible groups, teachers were also urged or required to have all students in a class read from the same on-grade-level book (previously called a reader, now called an anthology). Placing students in books that matched their reading ability has, in most places, become unacceptable. I won't try to describe flexible grouping here—the chapters of this book do that—but let me tell you one thing: It is not simple! Master teacher Regie Routman (see Chapter 5) indicates that it took her ten years to move from ability to flexible grouping, a reflection of its complexity.

Flexible grouping for reading instruction is not as simple as whole class or ability group instruction. But is it better? On the basis of visits to quite a few classrooms and conversations with many, many teachers, I am convinced—and the chapters in this book support this position—that in classrooms where flexible grouping is implemented effectively, the results are superb, far more positive than could be achieved with ability groups. Radencich and McKay (Chapter 5) do an excellent job of pointing to some of the wonderful benefits: increased self-esteem and positive attitudes on the part of students (this in and of itself compels us to work toward flexible grouping); easier integration of the curriculum; seeking out and using a much wider variety of reading materials; more effective use of volunteers, para-professionals, and special teachers; and more. It's wonderful to visit a classroom where flexible grouping is working. However, Radencich and McKay also point to some of the pitfalls that can occur when moving from ability grouping to flexible grouping; two that especially concern me are overuse of whole class instruction and a failure to meet the needs of both less proficient and highly proficient readers. Last year I visited a fourth-grade classroom of a teacher who had been required to move from ability to flexible groups and to place all students in grade-level anthologies. The reading lesson I observed was amazingly like the whole class, round-robin oral reading of the Dick-and-Jane era that I described earlier. This teacher had not been provided with the professional development experiences to move from ability to flexible grouping; in fact, he hadn't moved to flexible grouping but had moved from ability grouping to whole class instruction. Poor readers in this class were embarrassed in front of the whole class; talented readers were bored to distraction. Ability grouping would have been a better alternative than what I saw in this fourth-grade classroom. The teacher knew he and his students were having problems, but had no idea how to address them given the constraints he was teaching under.

This book, *Flexible Grouping for Literacy in the Elementary Grades*, is a superb starting point for teachers who are moving to or trying to improve the use of flexible grouping for reading instruction. The book is excellent in being both honest and practical. Its honesty is reflected in all of the chapters as they echo the position that organizing for instruction is challenging and complex. It requires a good knowledge base and decision-making abilities. Those who read the book to find a formula for flexible grouping or a quick fix of any kind will be disappointed.

Nevertheless, this is an enormously practical book. The editors, who also co-authored three of the chapters, build on the day-to-day experiences they've had in working with teachers to implement flexible grouping procedures. Chapters 3, 4, and 5 offer, not one model, but several models that have been implemented successfully. These chapters present detailed practical suggestions, but the strong message throughout is that these models and suggestions will need to be adapted, modified by each teacher to fit her or his teaching style and beliefs about literacy, in order to address successfully the needs of each of his or her students.

In Chapter 6, Paratore addresses the equally complex issue of the forms assessment should take in a classroom where flexible groups are employed. The chapter provides many helpful guidelines for linking assessment to instruction and for implementing a portfolio approach to assessment.

Chapter 7 by Cunningham addresses the problem of students who fail to learn to read in our educational system. Moving from ability to flexible grouping won't solve that problem. It requires a far more aggressive approach, an approach that shifts the emphasis from correcting and remediating to *preventing* reading problems—problems that have a devastating effect on the educational, social, and psychological well-being of children. As educators, we have a professional, even a moral, responsibility to promote—no, *force*—the implementation of programs like those described in this chapter.

I haven't mentioned the first chapter—a superb review by Barr of the research on grouping for instruction. I can't decide whether I think it better to read this chapter first or last. Read first, it serves as a superb framework for a thoughtful consideration of the chapters that follow; read last, it provides great justification for the cautious positions taken and the helpful suggestions offered in the other chapters. This comprehensive, even-handed review of the research on ability grouping makes it clear that studies on the effects of ability grouping on student achievement are equivocal at best. Though the research is inconclusive, Barr appropriately draws reasonable conclusions based on research, experience, and common sense. There are some dangers associated with ability grouping that need to be considered and addressed. We should be actively exploring, experimenting with, and critically evaluating alternatives to ability grouping. Although the use of permanent, static ability seems unwarranted, thoughtful, careful, and selected use of ability groups can, in fact, be advantageous. A superb summary statement within the chapter says:

> The main point in thinking about this literature on grouping is the inconclusiveness of the results . . . why we should expect more than inconsistent results is interesting. A social arrangement, of itself, does not lead directly to learning outcomes; rather, it is the instructional activities that students experience that influence what they learn and how they feel about it.

Changing from ability grouping to flexible grouping is no panacea for the challenges facing us as we try to ensure that every student in our schools will become literate. As the quotation suggests, the quality of the instruction that takes place is more important than the social arrangement itself. Although I wholeheartedly recommend that we thoughtfully reconsider our grouping policies, I worry that in many schools moving from ability to flexible grouping will be seen as a simple, easy transition. For some teachers it may be; for many it is not. *Flexible Grouping for Literacy in the Elementary Grades* is the best, most thorough, honest, and practical book on the topic. It is an excellent source of ideas and a starting point for change, but school administrators must be able to address frustrations and to problem-solve as colleagues.

Administrators and outside "experts" who expect instant, unsupported change from ability to flexible grouping fail to recognize the complexities facing many of today's teachers, who, in addition to moving from ability to flexible grouping, are also being expected to move forward in integrating the language arts, developing cross-curricular projects and activities, shifting from basal to literature-based reading instruction, replacing workbooks with "authentic" reading and writing experiences, increasing the use of multicultural and nonfiction literature, and implementing a portfolio approach to literacy assessment. The list could go on, and it only includes changes in literacy instruction/assessment. For all I know, there may be similar demands for changes in areas like math, science, and social studies; but, unlike the classroom teacher, I don't have to know about those areas—literacy is more than I can handle.

"Life sure was simpler in the days of Dick and Jane." However, I have no desire to return to that simplicity. More than ever before, many of us are honestly facing the reality that teaching and assessing literacy are challenging, messy activities requiring lots of hard work, thoughtful experimentation, and reasonable advice. The topic of grouping and organizing for reading instruction is one of those complex activities. I'm delighted that Radencich and McKay have assembled a rich, informative book that guides and challenges but doesn't present unrealistic panaceas.

Life in classrooms may have been simpler in the days of Dick and Jane, but it wasn't as good!

▶ Preface

In putting together *Flexible Grouping for Literacy in the Elementary Grades,* we have aimed to explore our commitment to the potential of flexible grouping. We see flexible grouping as grouping that is not static, where the members of reading groups and the types of reading groups change frequently. For example, students may work with a partner, in a small cooperative or teacher-directed group, or with the whole class. The basis for grouping may be students' interest or need. Often students are grouped heterogeneously. Typically, flexible grouping may revolve around a core grade-level selection read by an entire class or around an individualized trade book program. Teachers attempting flexible grouping recognize that reading achievement is a function not only of the text, but also of the conditions that surround the learning situation.

Because of the complexity of the issues of grouping, the chapters in this book cannot be self-contained. Educators who read *Flexible Grouping for Literacy in the Elementary Grades* as a whole will find information in one chapter that furthers understanding of previously read material.

In this book we have shared our experiences in two districts, how we got started, our implementation, and the impact of flexible grouping. We have called on outside experts to provide a perspective from a distance: Jack Pikulski to set the tone, Rebecca Barr for background, Wendy Kasten for literature circles, Pat Cunningham for addressing struggling students, Jeanne Paratore for an alternative model and for assessment, and Elfrieda Hiebert for reactions. All the authors encourage input from readers who are exploring the evolving concept of flexible grouping.

Acknowledgments

We are grateful

— to the many educators, students, and parents who have given of their precious time to educate children and whose ideas are an integral part of the writing in this book.
— to the teachers of Dade and Pinellas County classrooms who have allowed us to visit their classrooms and learn along with them.
— to the Dade and Pinellas County curriculum leadership, who have given us all the opportunity to take risks and grow professionally.
— to Sandra Shelton of the Anne M. Dorner Middle School in Ossining, New York; Robert Rude of Rhode Island College; and Carol V. Lloyd from the University of Nebraska at Omaha for their careful review of this manuscript.
— to Janie Guilbault and Mary Osborne, two Pinellas County writing demonstration lead teachers, whose coaching in the teaching of writing is an inspiration to all.

About the Authors and Contributors

Marguerite C. Radencich's Ph.D. in Education (Reading) is from the University of Miami. She has taught at the elementary and secondary school levels and has served as an elementary assistant principal. She is now the kindergarten to adult reading supervisor for Dade County Public Schools, Miami, Florida. She regularly teaches graduate reading courses. She serves on the editorial board of the *Journal of Reading* and the *Reading Research Quarterly* and also has served in this role for *The Reading Teacher*. Aside from her other publications for Allyn and Bacon, *Administration and Supervision of the Reading/Writing Program* and *Handbook for the K–12 Reading Resource Specialist* (co-authored), she is the author of numerous professional articles and co-author of two pieces of software published by Teacher Support Software, *The Semantic Mapper* and *The Literary Mapper,* and of two books published by Free Spirit, *How to Help Your Child with Homework* and *School Power—Strategies for School Success.*

Dr. Radencich is active with professional organizations. She has served as president of the Florida Reading Association and is currently president of the Reading Supervisors of Florida. She chairs the International Reading Association's Supervisors and Reading Special Interest Group.

Lyn McKay is a supervisor of elementary reading and language arts for Pinellas County Schools, Clearwater, Florida. She has a Ph.D. in Curriculum and Instruction with an emphasis in reading from the University of South Florida and an M.A. from Teachers College, Columbia University. She serves on the editorial board of the *Florida Reading Quarterly* and has recently served on the editorial board of *The Reading Teacher*. She frequently teaches graduate courses at the University of South Florida. Dr. McKay has given workshops and speeches at local, state, and national conferences sponsored by the International Reading Association, National Reading Conference, and Florida Reading Association. She was co-chair and presenter for an institute on Flexible Grouping at the 1991 International Reading Association National Conference in Las Vegas. Her doctoral study, *Extended Wait-Time and Its Effect on the Listening Comprehension of Kindergarten Students,* is published in the National Reading Conference Yearbook, 1987.

Dr. McKay chairs the Studies and Research Committee of the Florida Reading Association. In that role, she has edited the committee's annual publication, *Teachers on the Cutting Edge,* a series of research summaries on topics including flexible grouping, assessment, and multiage classrooms. She has served on many state committees, including chairing instructional materials councils and working on the Grade 4 Writing Assessment for Florida.

Rebecca Barr is a professor at the National College of Education, National-Louis University. For many years she has conducted research on the ways students are organized for classroom instruction and the consequences of these arrangements. On the basis of this study, she has written numerous articles and a book, *How Schools Work* (University of Chicago Press, 1983). During 1992–1993, she served as president of the National Reading Conference. Currently she serves on the editorial boards of the *Journal of Reading Behavior* and the *Reading Research Quarterly.*

Patricia Cunningham is a professor at Wake Forest University in Winston Salem, North Carolina. She has a B.A. from the University of Rhode Island, an M.A. from Florida State University, and a Ph.D. from the University of Georgia. In addition to university teaching, she worked for ten years in public school positions that included first-grade teacher, fourth-grade teacher, remedial reading teacher, curriculum coordinator, and director of reading. Dr. Cunningham has published numerous research and applied articles. For four years, she wrote "The Clip Sheet," a materials review column in *The Reading Teacher.* She also wrote a "Trends in Reading" column for *Educational Leadership* and a column for the intermediate teacher in *Reading Today.* Dr. Cunningham has co-authored several reading textbooks as well as *Phonics They Use: Words for Reading and Writing.* She and Richard Allington recently wrote a new book, *Classrooms That Work: They Can ALL Read and Write.* Dr. Cunningham's major interest is in finding alternative teaching strategies for students commonly classified as "at-risk."

Elfrieda H. Hiebert began her educational career as an elementary teacher in Clovis, California. After receiving the Ph.D. in Educational Psychology from the University of Wisconsin–Madison, she taught at the University of Kentucky and, more recently, at the University of Colorado–Boulder. Her research on the impact of instructional and assessment practices on literacy acquisition has been published in journals such as *American Educational Research Journal, Reading Research Quarterly,* and *Journal of Educational Psychology.* She has edited *Literacy for a Diverse Society* (1991), *Getting Reading Right from the Start: Effective Early Literacy Interventions* (1994, with Barbara Taylor), and *Authentic Reading Assessment: Practices and Possibilities* (1994, with Sheila Valencia and Peter Affierbach), and contributed to *Becoming a Nation of Readers* (1985), a national report on effective literacy practices. Professor Hiebert has been a recipient of a Spencer Fellowship awarded through the National Academy of Education. As an active member of professional organizations devoted to literacy, she edits the "Research Directions" column for *Language Arts*, serves on editorial boards such as the board of *The Elementary School Journal*, and served as the 1994 program chair for the Division on Instruction and Learning of the American Educational Research Association. Dr. Hiebert speaks frequently to teachers and works on reading and writing programs as an author of Silver Burdett Ginn's literacy program. She is currently Professor of Education at the University of Michigan.

Wendy C. Kasten was an elementary school teacher in Maine before completing her Ph.D. at the University of Arizona. She teaches language arts and children's literature, and is an active researcher in literacy issues and multiage teaching and learning at the University of South Florida at Sarasota. Currently at Kent State University, Dr. Kasten consults regularly and is first author of *The Multi-age Classroom: A Family of Learners* (R. C. Owen, 1993), *Building Families of Learners: Implementing Multi-age Classrooms* (R. C. Owen, 1994), and other educational articles.

Kay "Casey" Lustgarten, Ed.S., is a Chapter 1 Curriculum Specialist for Reading at West Little River Elementary in the Dade County (Miami) Public Schools and an adjunct instructor at Barry University. She has worked as a reading resource specialist for Frederick Douglass Elementary. She regularly presents at local workshops and at state and national conferences.

Pamela T. Moore has been with the Pinellas County School system for the past twenty-two years. She is currently serving as principal of Cypress Woods Elementary in Palm Harbor, Florida. Her background includes experiences as a classroom teacher, reading specialist, assistant principal, district-level reading and language arts supervisor, and elementary school principal. She holds the M.A. degree in reading education from the University of South Florida in Tampa, Florida.

Pat Nelms has been a supervisor of elementary reading and language arts for Pinellas County Schools, Clearwater, Florida, for eleven years. She was previously a school-based reading and language arts specialist for nine years. She has an M.A. in reading from the University of South Florida. In addition to her reading and language arts responsibilities, Mrs. Nelms is responsible for the nationally recognized elementary compensatory education program in the district. She has given workshops and speeches at local, state, national, and international conferences sponsored by the International Reading Association, Florida Reading Association, Florida Department of Education, and Florida Association of Supervision and Curriculum Development. She has served on state committees, including instructional materials councils and the advisory committee for Grade 4 Writing Assessment for Florida. She worked on a Florida state grant for developing reading objectives.

Jeanne R. Paratore is Associate Professor of Education at Boston University, where she teaches courses in literacy and language. Her current research interests are three: the study of family literacy and the implementation of family literacy programs with immigrant families; the study of portfolio assessment and its implementation in classroom settings; and instructing children in reading and writing within heterogeneously grouped classroom settings. Dr. Paratore's most recent publications are related to these three areas of research. She is also an author on a leading basal reading program and a frequent speaker at national and local conferences and professional development meetings.

Gloria L. Plaza is a Chapter 1 Reading Coordinator in the Dade County (Miami) Public Schools. Mrs. Plaza has a master's degree in Elementary Education and a Specialist degree in Reading. She has instructed kindergarten through fourth-grade students as a classroom teacher and a reading resource specialist. Mrs. Plaza has presented at local, state, and national conferences and conducts ongoing district workshops. She was honored as Teacher of the Year at Frederick Douglass Elementary.

▶ 1

What Research Says about Grouping in the Past and Present and What It Suggests about the Future

REBECCA BARR

We are currently evaluating our instructional grouping practices. Several factors seem to have precipitated this reexamination. Our increased understanding of the constructive nature of reading and the mutually supportive relation of reading and writing has led us to experiment with alternative forms of literacy instruction. We are finding not only that we need longer blocks of time to combine reading and writing instruction, but also that our interactive teaching strategies encourage and enable us to change the way we organize students for reading instruction. Students who would have had extreme difficulty understanding a selection can, with appropriate prereading instruction, now read with comprehension.

At the same time, a variety of cultural forces are at work. The past decade has been characterized by high rates of immigration; this has led to increased cultural and linguistic diversity among students. We are concerned about the de facto segregation that often results from ability grouping. Given these societal pressures as well as our newer ways of thinking about literacy

1

instruction, it is not surprising we are reconsidering the ways we group students for instruction and searching for new alternatives.

The purpose of this chapter is to provide a framework for thinking about issues of grouping. This reflective analysis is organized in four sections. In the first, I place ability grouping in the United States in historical perspective and consider ways in which other nations organize their students for instruction. In the second, I consider the traditional research literature and the more recent descriptive studies of ability grouping. The focus of the third section is on three forms of evidence that have had a significant impact on my thinking about ability grouping. In the final section, I consider grouping in the future and identify some important issues. In this discussion of grouping, I draw heavily on earlier reviews I have written (Barr, 1989a, 1989b, 1992; Barr & Dreeben, 1991).

GROUPING IN THE PAST IN THE UNITED STATES AND IN OTHER NATIONS

Historical Trends

Ability grouping for reading instruction is pervasive in U.S. schools (Austin & Morrison, 1963; Findley & Bryan, 1971; Goodlad, 1984). Ability groups within classes are common at all levels, particularly the primary; in addition, cross-class grouping arrangements (tracking) frequently occur in the intermediate grades and high schools. Grouping on the basis of ability or achievement has an interesting history. The tendency to regularize education was manifest in the Lancasterian schools in the early 1800s. Shortly thereafter, in the 1830s, a well-articulated curriculum and graded classes following those of Prussian schools were advocated by Horace Mann (Tyack, 1974). The first graded school in the United States, founded in Boston in 1847, was adopted during the next quarter century in all parts of the nation (Otto, 1932).

Curricular developments occurred at the same time as the development of graded schools. The first graded readers were probably written for the Lancasterian schools by Samuel Wood early in the nineteenth century (Venezky, 1988); those written by the McGuffeys and others followed. Thus, during the mid-1800s, the rapid expansion of schooling is associated with the grading of classes and reading materials.

As problems developed within age-graded classes because of significant differences among students, educators came to recognize the need to individualize instruction. One response was to form classes of students on the basis of similar academic progress. The first recorded example of ability grouping within grade levels occurred in the St. Louis schools in 1862, when

W. T. Harris was superintendent (Otto, 1932). Alternatively, in 1988, P. W. Search of Pueblo, Colorado, addressed the problem of large differences among students within classes by individualizing instruction.

In the late 1800s and early 1900s, new waves of immigration occurred, leading to a second period of expansion in schooling. This was also a period of great educational ferment, including the development of educational tests and the scientific study of learning. Individual differences within grades were widely recognized, and, in response, many new grouping plans were developed in such cities as Joplin, Denver, Detroit, Winnetka, and Gary. Although the plans differed in detail, each attempted to arrange students so that all would profit from instruction.

This was also the time when teachers first began forming small ability groupings *within* their classes for reading instruction. One of the earliest references to this practice occurred in the *Story Hour Readers Manual* (published by the American Book Company in 1913). The manual advised teachers to form separate groups for children who are "slow and need more assistance" and those who "progress rapidly."

Accompanying these changes in grouping were developments in curricular materials. Reading programs were simplified through the addition of preprimers at the lower levels. By limiting the number of new words introduced and repeating them, it was believed, stories could be made easier (Smith, 1965). The reading programs themselves became more comprehensive through the development of teacher's guides and student workbooks. For a second time, then, we see changes in the curriculum occurring along with those in grouping.

We are currently in a period similar to that of the early 1900s when educators faced increased diversity in the culture and language of students. As in earlier times, we are rethinking our extensive use of ability grouping and the appropriateness of other materials we use for reading and language arts. Yet, although conditions in the early 1900s led to the increased use of ability grouping, current conditions seem to be leading us away from ability grouping to other forms of social organization.

Cross-National Comparisons

The functions served by schools vary widely from nation to nation: education for the masses in some countries, in contrast to the formation of governing and social elites in others. As a result, different kinds of schools have developed from country to country. In the United States, for example, given its tradition of common schooling, elementary schools tend not to be distinguished by type. At the secondary level, comprehensive high schools are the norm, although differences occur in the type of curriculum (vocational versus academic.).

British education outwardly resembles U.S. schools in certain ways, but through a different set of historical circumstances. The "streaming" in the British lower schools, for example, represents an approach similar to some forms of tracking in U.S. schools. In addition, private schools attended mainly by members of the social elite provide a form of stratification more prominent in Britain than in the United States. Differentiation in Britain, as in Europe, occurs also through the development of different types of schools, particularly at the secondary level. Thus, in one way or another, it is assumed in most Western nations that instruction can be most effectively provided when students are grouped on the basis of ability.

In contrast, instruction in Asian countries follows a somewhat different pattern (Stevenson & Stigler, 1992; Stigler & Stevenson, 1991). In Japan, common schooling occurs through the ninth grade. A cluster of societal conditions in Japan (high rates of kindergarten attendance, late marriage age, a low divorce rate, a small proportion of mothers working outside the home, relative income equality compared to the industrial West, and ethnic homogeneity) supports equity in educational opportunity through undifferentiated elementary schools and classrooms (Rohlen, 1983; Brinton, 1988). As Cummings (1980) writes:

> Under no circumstances do the teachers consciously form groups stratified by ability as is the practice in growing numbers of American schools. Although the teachers recognize differences in ability among their students, they feel it is their responsibility as public school teachers in a democratic society to try to bring all the students up to a common level. (p. 127)

Japanese schools do, however, confront the problems of diversity by different means, such as a slow instructional pace, out-of-school tutoring, and parental involvement through home instruction (Mason, Anderson, Omura, Uchida, & Imai, 1989).

Mason and her colleagues describe this style of instructional support as "deep reading." Historically, the rereading of selections is valued, as embodied in an old Japanese saying: "Read it again and again and you will realize its meaning" (Mason et al., 1989, p. 401). Oral reading is the preferred route to comprehension; silent reading occurs rarely. Japanese teachers describe deep reading as "becoming sensitive to the nuances in slightly different forms of expressions, understanding the feelings of characters at a subtle level, appreciating the social or historical context in which stories are placed, learning to read between the lines, capturing the writer's motif, having personal reactions to stories, and connecting stories to one's inner, subjective world" (Mason et al., 1989, p. 403). This approach contrasts with the reading instruction experienced by most first and second graders in the

United States. Even more striking, local and national standardized reading tests are not used in Japanese elementary or secondary schools (Gunderson, personal communication, November 22, 1993).

Stevenson and his colleagues also describe the highly interactive nature of Japanese literacy and mathematics instruction (Stevenson, Lee, Stigler, Kitamura, Kimura, & Kato, 1988; Stevenson & Stigler, 1992; Stigler & Stevenson, 1991). They characterize lessons as coherent units, with beginnings, middles, and endings, that focus on single problems or themes. White (1987) describes Japanese teachers who repeat lessons as many times as necessary, in a step-by-step fashion; they do not expect children to grasp new principles or approaches thoroughly at first. Indeed, children often stated the point of a lesson before the teacher (White, 1987). Despite this thoughtful, slow-paced mode of instruction, Japanese children's reading achievement appears to be similar to that of U.S. children (Stevenson & Lee, 1990; Stevenson & Stigler, 1992).

Japanese education is, however, not perfect. Instructional emphases change drastically when students enter middle and high schools. The slow-paced, nontracked literacy instruction of the early elementary schools is followed by later instruction in secondary schools that differ from each other in terms of academic performance (Rohlen, 1983). Exams for university entrance cause adolescents considerable anxiety because students' performance on these exams strongly influences the type of university they can attend and their access to prestigious jobs later on. Factual learning largely determines how well students do on the entrance exam; accordingly, the demands of the exam shape instruction in middle and high schools. It is as if two different models exist in Japan: one of early schooling that focuses on the importance of cooperation and deep understanding, and a second one where factual learning is emphasized in preparation for the university entrance exam.

From the vantage point of current educational practice, it is easy to see how grouping both within and between schools has been understood as a mechanism for dealing with diverse school populations in Western nations. Asian education, and the Japanese case in particular, challenge the assumption that ability grouping is the only way to respond to diversity, thus providing an alternative view of instruction.

RESEARCH ON ABILITY GROUPING

Traditional Studies

What does the research literature tell us about ability grouping? Is it necessary? Can it be justified? What are other viable ways to organize students for instruction? Since the early decades of the century researchers have asked about the implications of ability grouping for how much students learn and how they feel about themselves as learners. The typical research design is to compare the learning of students grouped for instruction on the basis of ability or achievement with that of similar students receiving instruction in more diverse groups.

The literature is characterized by two major waves of reviews, the first in the early 1930s and the second in the 1960s. Reviewers from both periods criticized the adequacy of the research undertaken and emphasized the equivocal and inconsistent results that appeared from study to study. Yet, there were major differences in conclusions from these two periods of reviewers. For example, a substantial number of the early reviewers concluded that ability grouping benefited "slow" students (e.g., Miller & Otto, 1930; Whipple, 1936). Many from the second wave, in contrast, discerned a tendency for homogeneously grouped high achievers to learn more than comparable students in diverse groups; in contrast, low achievers were seen as doing less well in homogeneous than heterogeneous groups (e.g., Eash, 1961; Esposito, 1973; Findley & Bryan, 1971).

Recent Analyses

Several recent analyses have also been made of the existing body of grouping studies (see, for example, Barr & Dreeben, 1991; Hiebert, 1983; Kulik & Kulik, 1982; Noland, 1985). I find the summary of this literature by Slavin (1987) to be particularly useful because he distinguishes studies of ability grouping *within* classes from those of various forms of ability grouping *between* classes, and studies involving reading are treated separately from those focusing on other subject areas.

With regard to ability groups within classes for reading instruction, Slavin found no studies that met his criteria. That is, he located no research in which the learning of students in small ability groups within classes was compared with that of students receiving total class instruction in non-ability-grouped classes. This was probably because of the pervasive use of some form of ability grouping for reading instruction in most U.S. classrooms. Thus, he found no basis for evaluating this practice in reading. He did, however, find that instruction was more effective for intermediate math when students were grouped on the basis of ability than when they were not so grouped. Although this finding may also hold for reading, we lack evidence to support it.

With regard to ability grouping between classes, Slavin found students from classes formed on the basis of ability did not learn more than similar students from heterogeneous classes. This result may reflect that many of the heterogeneous classes may have been subdivided into small ability groups within classes. Regrouping students across classes *within* grade level for reading instruction did not lead to higher achievement, but regrouping students *between* grade levels did. Both lower achieving and higher achieving students were found to learn more when they were instructed in cross-grade groups than did similar students instructed in self-contained classrooms. This finding may have come about because some talented younger students were exposed to very challenging work and were able to learn a great deal from it, and because more individual support was given to lower achieving students.

In reflecting on the results from the literature on grouping, perhaps the main point to remember is their inconclusiveness. Ability grouping has not been found clearly advantageous. More important, it is interesting that we expected anything other than inconsistent results. A social arrangement, ability grouping or any other, does not lead in any direct fashion to learning. Rather, the activities in which children participate, the materials they read and write, and the teaching support they experience shape what they learn and their feelings about it.

Instructional Differences between Reading Groups

A more recent set of studies examines grouping from a somewhat different perspective, asking about the quality of the instruction students receive in ability groups. Since groups are composed to facilitate differential instruction, the finding by researchers that instruction differs between high and low groups is not surprising. Reviewers such as Allington (1983), Barr (1989a, 1989b), Hiebert (1983), and Pikulski (1991) summarize the results from this research as follows: The instruction of children in low groups tends to include a greater number of intrusions and less time on task than that of students in higher achieving groups. Low-group members tend to read less material, work on less complex assignments, and receive instruction that emphasizes smaller units of print and decoding, rather than meaning. They experience more drill and skill work, read aloud more often, and tend to be asked questions requiring recall rather than reasoning. They are provided with different prompts from teachers and more structured activities with advanced organizers than are students in higher achieving groups. Although some instructional researchers also claim low-group members receive less instructional time (Hunter, 1978), others have not found differential time allocations (Barr, 1992; Collins, 1986; Weinstein, 1976).

This set of evidence often leads reviewers to the conclusion that students in low groups are being treated unfairly. Some even conclude that the nature of their instruction has caused the students to be poor readers. There are problems in reaching such conclusions. First, most of the case studies focus only on instruction and fail to describe the learning of students in a systematic fashion. Without this vital evidence on learning, it is inappropriate to draw conclusions about the consequences of instruction for it. Second, unless low groups receive and respond positively to instruction that is similar to that provided high-group members, it cannot be known for certain the same treatment would be appropriate. Yet, it is reasonable to conclude from this set of findings that students in low groups experience instruction that differs in important respects from that of high-group members, and their instruction may be viewed as inferior given our current views on "best practice" (Anderson, Hiebert, Scott, & Wilkinson, 1985).

PERSONAL REFLECTIONS ON GROUPING RESEARCH

What sense should we make of the research on ability grouping? We know several things. Ability grouping in one form or another pervades schools in the United States. Because of its pervasiveness, studies have tended to compare one form of ability grouping with other forms, to reach equivocal and inconsistent results.

The question not answered about reading instruction is whether there is any advantage to the use of ability groups. As discussed earlier, there seem to be no well-controlled studies of reading instruction without ability groups to address this issue (Slavin, 1987). The more recent descriptive literature comparing high and low reading groups is useful in identifying instructional differences, but the forms of instruction characteristic of high-group instruction are rarely tried with low groups; learning outcomes typically are not measured. We currently lack evidence from systematic research to guide our practice. Yet, evidence does exist that has had a marked influence on the philosophy of ability grouping. In this section, evidence is organized in the form of three questions: Is the instruction of low and high groups really different? Are members of low and high groups different in their reading abilities? How do low-group members feel about their reading experiences?

Is the Instruction of Low and High Groups Really Different?

One stated purpose for separating children into reading groups on the basis of their achievement is to offer them more appropriate instruction. If we should find instead that the instruction of different reading groups is highly similar, what would it mean? Some of the research reviewed in the prior section revealed a number of differences in the instruction received by high- and low-group members. Other evidence suggests an alternative view. Because of a concern for the inadequate reading skill of many low-group members, reviewers have focused on these differences to demonstrate the unequal and unfair way these students are treated. This focus, however, may have blinded us to similarities characterizing the instruction of low- as well as high-group members. A key similarity: Most elementary school students in a class or school read from the same reading programs. Both low-group and high-group members are assigned the same stories and experience many of the same activities, although at somewhat different times during the year (Chall & Squires, 1991). It has been reported that low groups receive less instructional time (Allington, 1983), but if we look within individual classes, we find all groups receive about the same amount (Barr, 1992).

Even the claim that the pace of instruction differs may not be true, except during the first six months of instruction. A study undertaken in twelve first-grade classrooms found that low groups in all classes spent considerably more time than higher groups on the first book, usually the first preprimer (Barr, 1992; Barr, Chen, & Dreeben, 1991). High groups, on average, spent about six weeks; low groups, about fourteen weeks. Thereafter, there appeared to be little difference between low and high groups in the number of weeks they took; both groups took an average of six or seven weeks on the next two books, and ten weeks on the fourth book, usually the primer.

While low-group members were completing the fourth book, however, high-group members completed the final book of first grade and sometimes read from the second-grade reader. High groups were capable of proceeding at a faster pace, but second-grade teachers often did not want first graders to read too much of the second-grade basal. For this reason, first-grade instruction of the high group was made less demanding. At the same time, low-group members were brought along at a pace that resulted in reading materials that may have been at their frustration level. However appropriate or inappropriate, this evidence suggests the main difference between low and high groups is one of minor difference in the pace of instruction. This difference is established early in first grade when the first book is read. Children progress at about the same pace thereafter—a pace too slow for high-group members and too fast for those students who encounter difficulty learning to read.

A study of fourth-grade groups revealed similar findings (Barr & Sadow, 1989), and focused on the instruction of seven different teachers. In each case, low groups tended to read at the same or even higher levels from the basal than did higher-achieving groups from the same classes. For example, the low group in Teacher 3's class read one and a half grade levels of the basal, while the high group completed just one grade level. Even more astounding, Teacher 4's low group completed two grade levels; the high group completed one (Barr & Sadow, 1989, p. 58).

On the basis of my work with teachers in other schools, these results are fairly typical. Given the structure of the basal programs, it is not unusual for students in low groups to proceed about a half-year behind average group members, and those in high groups about a half-grade ahead. The differences arising during the first half of first grade continue to characterize the discrepancy between high and low groups during the rest of elementary schooling.

Combining evidence from the first- and fourth-grade studies, we begin to see that the instruction of low- and high-group members is similar: They read the same stories and participate in similar instructional activities. Even the pace of instruction is similar after the beginning months of first grade. Because of this early pace difference, high-group members continue to read about one grade level ahead of low-group members in the basal program.

Note we are talking about *instruction,* not learning. Though both groups are similar in the instruction they receive, the amount of learning differs: High-group members show higher levels of learning than what would be expected on the basis of instruction, and low-group members often show lower (Barr & Dreeben, 1983). As far as their instruction is concerned, I argue that the difference between students in low and high groups is minor. Students are labelled through low- and high-group membership, but offered instruction that is essentially the same. Moreover, at the intermediate levels, materials at adjacent grade levels do not differ that much in the challenge presented to students, including those who are lower in achievement (Homan, Hines, & Kromrey, 1993). Instead, I believe that either students should be taught in diverse groups or the class should be instructed as a whole, offering differential support as necessary. *Or,* if the practice of ability grouping continues, teachers must truly individualize instruction so major benefits through greater instructional support occur for the student labelled "low-group member."

Are Members of Low and High Groups Different in Their Reading?

A second piece of evidence pertains to the composition of reading groups. I have found through my studies of group composition that first-grade children in reading groups have similar ability to read stories and other textual materials, but children from different groups differ greatly in their reading proficiency. That is, children in lower groups simply are unable to read stories read by the middle- and high-group members because they have not yet developed sufficient skill with print.

Because of this experience, I was unprepared for what was found in seven fourth-grade classes when plotting the reading comprehension scores of group members (Barr & Sadow, 1989). We began by looking at the group composition in the classrooms of two teachers from one school, School A. Reading instruction was departmentalized; Teacher 1 had the higher group and Teacher 2, the lower group. With the exception of a small number of students, 18 percent, the two groups overlapped completely in their comprehension skill as measured by the *Degrees of Reading Power* test. As we looked at groups in other schools and other classes, we found the teachers who grouped students by ability within classes also had groups that were highly overlapping in reading comprehension. In one class, Teacher 3 from School B, the high and low groups overlapped entirely.

Teachers 5 and 6 from School C organized students into four groups between them. With the exception of a single child, the four groups overlapped almost completely in comprehension. A similar pattern occurred for the three groups in Teacher 7's class. Only one of the seven teachers established extremely different, nonoverlapping groups: Teacher 4 had the highest and the lowest fourth-grade readers from School B. These findings suggest, contrary to what most believe, that there are many students with strong comprehension in low groups and many with quite poor comprehension in high groups.

How might this come about? It seems quite possible that groups, established in kindergarten or first grade on the basis of decoding skill and behavior, are perpetuated into later grades where background knowledge and comprehension are more important. Since decoding and listening comprehension are not strongly correlated, it might be expected that groups would grow more varied in comprehension as students become fluent readers. Further confirmation of this set of findings is needed, but other studies report similar results. When students are grouped on the basis of prior achievement, or on the basis of a single test, they will show considerable overlap on other similar measures of achievement (see Burr, 1931; Hartill, 1936; West, 1933). This evidence raises questions about ability groups in the intermediate grades. Through our grouping procedures, are we labeling students as poor readers who are, in fact, good comprehenders? More importantly, this evidence shows that fourth-grade teachers are able to teach groups diverse in comprehension. In sum, ability groups are highly overlapping in achievement, yet we tend to think group members are different and may, on this basis, expect different behavior and achievement.

The Feelings of Low-Group Members

A final piece of evidence pertains to the feelings of low-group members. One of the advantages of my interest in classroom instruction has been the opportunity to interact with children from many different classes at various points during the school year. All first graders with whom I have worked have been excited about being in first grade, and mainly so because of the prospect of learning how to read. By the end of the school year, some have had their confidence eroded. They are not sure the school game they have been playing is a fair one.

The enthusiasm and trust displayed by first graders, even those not well prepared for first grade, are rarely seen among low-group members in later grades. What is clear is that they have lost confidence in their ability to learn and have begun to dislike reading. Juel (1988) describes the feelings of students she followed from first to fourth grade. To judge how well they liked reading, questions were posed such as, "What would you rather do, read or watch TV?" One low-achieving fourth grader reported he "would rather clean the mold around the bathtub than read" (p. 442).

The discomfort of low-group members increases as they progress through the grades. The comments of a student entering a junior high school, but assigned to the "basic" track, illustrates the despair that can come from the extreme segregation of tracking (from Schafer & Olexa, 1971):

> I felt good when I was with my [elementary] class, but when they went and separated us—that changed us. That changed our ideas, our thinking, the way we thought about each other, and turned us into enemies toward each other—because they said I was dumb and they were smart. (pp. 62–63)

Most of us strive to develop students who not only can read well, but also who enjoy reading. It is doubtful that placing all children who encounter difficulty in the same class or instructional group represents sound instructional policy. The practice certainly does not develop students who love to read or who feel good about themselves as readers. Thus, the final type of evidence I consider in evaluating the merits of ability grouping is the impact of the practice on the affective development of students.

Summary

The results from comparative and descriptive studies summarized earlier are inconsistent and contradictory. Yet, as discussed in this section, I believe the evidence is sufficient to cause us to reflect on the need for ability grouping and to consider new alternatives. Compelling evidence comes from descriptions of those practices and from student comments, both of which challenge the practice of ability grouping. If we are serious about our goal of having all students love reading, ability groups would seem to be counterproductive.

And indeed, as we shall see in the next section, exploration of alternative forms of grouping is already underway. Recent studies not only show it is possible to use more flexible forms of grouping, they also provide a view of how these alternatives work.

GROUPING IN THE FUTURE:
THE CHALLENGE FACING US

What questions are researchers currently asking about grouping? While ability grouping was a popular topic for research in the 1980s, the most striking trend recently is that many educational researchers have lost interest in grouping as an issue. There are fewer studies now of ability grouping than before. Those being conducted tend to cluster into three main areas. The first set of case studies continues to explore what occurs in traditional classrooms where students are ability grouped (Purcell-Gates & Dahl, 1991). This work, which goes beyond earlier research to document the perceptions of participants, shows how teacher expectations and perceptions of students are adversely affected by the ability grouping arrangement (Barton, 1991).

A second set of studies concerns students with special learning needs (learning disabled, bilingual, gifted) and the implications of more flexible forms of instruction for them (Johnson, 1992; Kameenui, 1993; Lim & Watson, 1993; Scala, 1993). Focus on learning in groups with special needs, particularly the gifted, arises in part from the fear that all forms of differentiated instruction may be eliminated (Dooley, 1993).

A third set explores flexible forms of instruction and their implications for the organization of students. Some researchers expected to see more flexible forms of grouping in classrooms, but did not always find it (see Harrison, 1989, with respect to the Coalition schools). Other researchers, in contrast, report reduction or elimination of ability grouping (see Hart's 1989 study of schools implementing the Paideia Proposal).

The majority of studies reporting more flexible forms of grouping involve the implementation of instructional approaches based on a whole language philosophy (Bruneau, 1992; Dahl, 1993; Freepon, 1991; Morrow, 1992; Stice & Bertrand, 1992). In most of these, the focus is not on ability grouping per se, but flexible forms of grouping are described, including some classes and groups formed on the basis of ability. Flexible grouping arrangements—small heterogeneous groups, total class discussions, partner reading, groups based on strategy needs—are selected because they enable certain forms of communication to occur. Students report that they enjoy the whole language literacy experiences they are engaged in (Oldfather, 1993).

This body of work is useful in considering flexible forms of instructional grouping. At the same time, other issues must be considered. Some teachers' questions: If I want to move away from more rigid forms of ability grouping, where do I begin? Do I have to eliminate ability groups entirely? Does the stage at which children are in their reading development have a bearing on how they should be organized for literacy instruction? Pikulski (1991) cautions against a radical change in approach. Instead, he recommends a gradual incorporation of new instructional components that involve more flexible forms of grouping (see also Flood, Lapp, Flood, & Nagel, 1992). A range of alternative groupings may include grouping on the basis of achievement. Two important considerations in using any form of ability grouping: What is the instructional goal it serves? How can it be kept from becoming a rigid system?

There is a growing consensus in the field of literacy that, from the earliest years of schooling, reading and writing must be understood as a means to communicate with others and solve problems. At the same time, instructional activities in the earliest years, when children are learning about the nature of print, differ from later years when they are fluent readers. An issue of central importance during the early years: How much do children learn about the nature of print as they read and write? Is systematic instruction focused on print, and its relation to speech, useful? Is it necessary for some children? Do materials need to be carefully selected so they are appropriate in difficulty?

Greater problems may be associated with the total elimination of ability grouping in the primary grades before students develop fluency with print, than in later years. Reading groups may be useful because children with similar knowledge about print and reading proficiency can be provided supportive instruction focused on the relations between spelling and speech. Research shows that such instruction helps children, particularly those anticipated to encounter difficulty learning to read, to hear sounds in words, and to map the relationship between sounds and letters (Adams, 1990; Eldredge, 1991; Uhry & Shepherd, 1993).

Ability grouping also makes it easier for teachers to ensure that children interact with materials they can read with ease. Fluency develops through repeated practice with textual selections that pose few problems. Individuals differ in the amount of practice they need to achieve automaticity, but with sufficient contextual practice most can become fluent readers.

Alternatively, some recent research shows that when teachers modify their instructional strategies to include support for reading literature and informational passages, and when writing is a major component of instruction and learning, a close match between the demands of text and children's knowledge about print may be less important (Homan, Hines, & Kromrey, 1993). Because of lingering uncertainties, I distinguish primary-grade instruction from intermediate instruction. For primary-grade instruction, I suggest two alternative models.

Primary Grades

In most primary classrooms we have grouped children on the basis of the amount of practice they need, but then we have provided them with the same amount of instructional time for practice (Barr, 1992). In spite of this, after the first preprimer, low groups and high groups proceed at about the same pace in the same amount of instructional time. Those low-group members who need more practice time are not given it. Rather, they proceed to new selections that are difficult for them because they have not had sufficient practice with the previous reading materials.

To remedy some of the failings of our current instructional approaches, two alternative models have merit. One model involves the use of small ability groups, with the goal of bringing low-group members up to the class average. The other model eliminates stable forms of ability grouping and uses alternative forms of instruction to facilitate the learning of all class members.

Instruction with Ability Groups.   With respect to the first model, existing evidence suggests that if we provide low-group members more instructional support and time for practice, they can achieve at a level similar to other class members. For example, in the research evaluating Reading Recovery methods, children are challenged with the next level of material once they show mastery of the prior level (Clay, 1985; Pinnell, 1989). Most children participating in this tutorial instruction achieve in the average range when tutoring is discontinued. If they are then subsequently grouped with the middle group, they continue to make adequate progress. That is, the tutorial intervention may minimize or avoid the development of an initial difference in reading between low- and high-group members (see also Wasik & Slavin, 1993). Similar results have been shown for small-group Chapter 1 instruction (Hiebert, Colt, Catto, & Gury, 1992).

Naturalistic class comparisons also provide support for the belief that if first graders are given more time for reading, they are able to make average progress in learning to do it (Dreeben & Barr, 1988). Teachers provide more instructional time for low-group members by including more low-group reading instruction time and using it well—adding a small-group meeting in the afternoon for students who need more time, and/or establishing partner reading in the afternoon when middle- and high-group members reread basal stories with low-group members.

The quality of small-group instruction needs to be enhanced to increase the opportunities low-group members have to learn (Duffy, 1993; Taylor, Short, Frye, & Shearer, 1992). Low-group members need more opportunities to read and to develop reading strategies. For example, round-robin reading allows for each child to experience only a limited amount of reading; in contrast, reading in unison or reading as partners gives each child a much greater opportunity to read. Small groups can become places where students discuss and reflect on their reading strategies.

Supported forms of writing need to become a main component of instruction. Although other students in a class may write easily and independently, some children need to see the writing process demonstrated through the use of sound boxes (Clay, 1985) and other forms of shared writing.

Yet, when ability groups are used, a major problem results: How can time when students are not working directly with the teacher best be put to use? Cunningham (1991) recommends three criteria for seatwork: It must relate to reading and writing; it must be an activity where a student needs to practice; and, it must be possible for the child to complete it successfully. She recommends several alternative activities, including independent reading of material the child has selected, daily writing, and working with a partner on worksheets. The author also discusses useful ways in which these alternatives can be implemented.

Supported reading of children in ability groups should constitute only one component of the literacy program. When children are reading literature and writing, more flexible forms of organization should be used, including total class instruction, small heterogeneous groups, and partner reading, in the beginning stages of literacy as well as later.

A final caution: When ability groups are formed to read selections from the basal, there is a greater chance rigid forms of ability grouping will become established. Informal observation suggests that literature-based ability groups are being used more flexibly, perhaps because selection of group members is based not only on reading ability, but also interest. One method some teachers using basals employ to avoid rigid group membership is to move children upward as they acquire reading proficiency and eliminate ability groups once children achieve some degree of fluency.

Instruction without Stable Ability Groups.   The second model involves eliminating stable ability grouping altogether in favor of ad hoc groupings such as heterogeneous small-group instruction, partner reading, and whole-class instruction. Some research has been undertaken on the effectiveness of these alternatives. Eldredge and Butterfield (1984, 1986), for example, compared second graders using a traditional basal in ability groups with those instructed in heterogeneous groups. Since the same reading selections were used for all students in the innovative classes, instruction was modified to involve peer-supported oral reading for the poorer readers. No achievement or attitudinal differences were found between students experiencing the two forms of instruction. In other words, there were no negative consequences due to the innovative arrangement.

Case-study research also provides suggestive evidence that whole-class instruction without traditional ability groups is feasible at the first-grade level. Earlier we referred to the Japanese study by Mason, Anderson, Omura, Uchida, and Imai (1989). They describe the early literacy experiences of young Japanese children based on visits to about 40 kindergarten and primary-grade classes. They found that Japanese classes are larger than those of U.S. schools, typically containing about 36 to 40 students, and as previously noted, whole-class instruction is used almost exclusively.

As described earlier, the pace of instruction was extremely slow, with an emphasis on deep reading to achieve the meaning of literature. A first-grade textbook, for example, might contain only nine stories and six exposi-tions. Mason et al. (1989) speculated about the reasons for the slow pace:

> One possible reason for the slow pace of instruction is that the goals of reading instruction in the typical Japanese classroom differ from those in the typical U.S. classroom . . . A second possible reason . . . is a need to accommodate less advanced children within the frame-work of whole-class lessons. (p. 397)

They note further that Japanese educators believe repeated oral reading is particularly valuable for children whose reading is least well developed. Mason and colleagues (1989) suggest that several factors may influence the success of this approach, such as the strong early reading proficiency of Japanese children and strong home support for learning. They also note the positive influences of kindergarten experiences, whole-class instruction, and the practice of deep reading in promoting literacy. They are concerned, how-ever, about the slow instructional pace for Japanese children with above-average ability.

Cunningham (Chapter 7; see also Cunningham, Hall, & Defee, 1991) describes a similar form of total-class first-grade instruction, but one with four thirty-minute periods devoted to literacy instruction. Some of the lower-achieving children encountered difficulty with the rapid pace of basal sto-ries; thus, they and other class members participated in a special oral read-ing group which met fifteen minutes each day. This incorporation of a modi-fied form of ability grouping suggests we may have difficulty avoiding it entirely, particularly in first grade and when students in a class differ greatly in reading skill.

Evidence on the effectiveness of whole language classes is beginning to emerge. Although the results from such studies reveal the effectiveness of reading and writing experience for many students (Morrow, 1992; Klesius, Griffith, & Zielonka, 1991), Hiebert (1991) expresses concern about students who encounter difficulty learning to read. Hiebert's studies of whole lan-guage classes observed that some children seemed to need more structured forms of instruction to progress well. These findings, if replicated, suggest we may need to provide greater degrees of structure and support for those children who experience difficulty learning to read. Alternatively, those chil-dren who learn easily thrive on self-selected literacy activities and need less support. Children initially needing high degrees of support, once they have progressed beyond the beginning stages of learning about print, may well profit from more self-selected activities and may need less instructional support.

Intermediate Grades

Since we seem to be teaching diverse groups in the intermediate grades, the disbanding of ability groups at this level would seem to be possible. Already some research and descriptive case studies are appearing in the literature that attest to the feasibility of using cooperative groups and other forms of heterogeneous grouping at the intermediate levels, in spite of diversity within classes (see Chapters 3, 4, and 6). Yet, more flexible forms of grouping, including ability grouping, may still be needed at the intermediate level to accommodate the range of reading levels in highly diverse classes.

The coordination of reading and writing enables students to learn new concepts through receptive and expressive means. This is particularly important when new understandings about people and things are being acquired. This coordination, however, typically demands longer time periods. Such longer periods can be found through elimination of reading groups and adoption of total-class modes of instruction. An advantage of total-class instruction is that it permits the use of more flexible forms of grouping such as reading partners, book clubs, and play-writing groups (Hoyt, 1992; Beyersdorfer & Schauer, 1993). Although systematic studies comparing innovative instruction with traditional forms of reading instruction are few in number, recent case studies indicate the feasibility of such instruction (see Keegan & Shrake, 1991; Swift, 1993).

Similarly, the use of pre- and postreading strategies makes reading selections accessible to a broader range of students. During prereading, central concepts are discussed, information about the topic is shared, and students establish a purpose for reading a selection (see Pardo & Raphael, 1991). Students, who without preparation may have had extreme difficulty understanding a selection, can read with comprehension following it. Consequently, it is possible for teachers to form more diverse groups or to abandon ability grouping entirely when prereading and postreading support are provided.

Studies that involve cooperative peer groups as part of reading instruction show that reading achievement is not negatively affected by the use of diverse peer groups, and is often enhanced (Rosenholz & Cohen, 1983). Further, in all of the experimental studies reviewed by Slavin (1983), achievement was enhanced through the inclusion of peer-group work. Similarly, a field study (Stevens, Madden, Slavin, & Farnish, 1987) showed higher achievement for students working in peer groups than individually. Often peer groups or work with partners takes the place of less-productive seatwork practice. Yet, the quality of the interaction in cooperative groups, whether negative or positive, influences student feelings about the groups and their learning (Battistich, Solomon, & Delucchio, 1993).

We are at a point when more systematic studies comparing the results of instruction with and without ability groups are beginning to appear. Teachers may well make a central contribution to this literature by describing the instruction, learning, and perceptions of students in new social arrangements and comparing them with those from a previous year, when more traditional forms of ability-grouped instruction were used.

CONCLUDING REMARKS

Ability grouping for reading instruction is pervasive in U.S. schools; it is common in most other nations as well. Japanese elementary schools represent a major exception to this pervasive tendency. All Japanese students are grouped heterogeneously into classes and receive the same instruction.

What are the advantages of grouping students on the basis of ability? The point in thinking about traditional research literature is the inconclusiveness of its results. Ability grouping has not been shown to be clearly advantageous in terms of learning outcomes. More recent descriptive studies comparing high and low reading groups show that low-group members receive instruction that is inferior given our current notions of "best practice." Yet, at the same time, the reading instruction of groups is quite similar: All groups read the same basal materials and perform similar reading and writing activities.

On the basis of the evidence presented, we currently lack evidence from systematic research to guide our practice. At the same time, sufficient evidence does exist leading us to reevaluate current ability-grouping practices and to experiment with new alternatives. Compelling evidence comes from descriptions of current practices and student comments, both of which challenge the practice of ability grouping. If we are serious about our goal to have all students love reading, ability groups would seem to be counterproductive.

We are entering a phase in U.S. schooling that promises many new developments in how students are organized for reading instruction. Because of the current pervasive use of ability groups and the difficulty inherent in changing established teaching practice (Barksdale-Ladd & Thomas, 1993; Pace, 1992; Pikulski, 1991), it can be anticipated that change will be slow. Greater problems may be associated with the total elimination of ability grouping in the primary grades before students develop fluency with print, than in later years. Nevertheless, as described in the final section of the chapter, the equivocal evidence on the effectiveness of ability groups and the harmful affective effects of ability groups have already led researchers and teachers to experiment with alternatives. We are beginning to build a body of knowledge on new ways to organize and instruct students in the areas of reading and writing.

REFERENCES

Adams, M. J. (1990). *Beginning to read: Thinking and learning about print.* Cambridge, MA: MIT Press.

Anderson, R. C., Hiebert, E. H., Scott, J. A., & Wilkinson, I. A. (1985). *Becoming a nation of readers.* Washington, DC: National Institute of Education.

Allington, R. (1983). The reading instruction provided readers of differing reading ability. *Elementary School Journal, 83,* 548–559.

Austin, M., & Morrison, C. (1963). *The first R: The Harvard report on reading in the elementary school.* New York: Macmillan.

Barksdale-Ladd, M. A., & Thomas, K. F. (1993). Eight teachers' reported pedagogical dependency on basal readers. *Elementary School Journal, 94*(1), 49–72.

Barr, R. (1989a). The social organization of literacy instruction. In S. McCormick & J. Zutell (Eds.), *Cognitive and social perspectives for literacy research and instruction* (pp. 19–33). Thirty-eighth Yearbook of the National Reading Conference. Chicago: National Reading Conference.

Barr, R. (1989b). Social organization of reading instruction. In C. Emilhovich (Ed.), *Locating learning across the curriculum: Ethnographic perspectives on classroom research* (pp. 57–86). Norwood, NJ: Ablex.

Barr, R. (1992). Teachers, materials and group composition in literacy instruction. In M. J. Dreher & W. H. Slater, *Elementary school literacy: Critical issues* (pp. 27–50). Norwood, MA: Christopher-Gordon.

Barr, R., Chen, R., & Dreeben, R. (1991). *The pace of first grade reading groups.* Unpublished manuscript.

Barr, R., & Dreeben, R. (1991). Grouping students for reading instruction. In R. Barr, M. Kamil, P. Mosenthal, & P. D. Pearson (Eds.), *Handbook of reading research* (Vol. 2, pp. 885–910). New York: Longman.

Barr, R., & Dreeben, R. [with Wiratchai, N.]. (1983). *How schools work.* Chicago: University of Chicago Press.

Barr, R., & Sadow, M. (1989). Influence of basal programs on fourth-grade reading instruction. *Reading Research Quarterly, 24,* 44–71.

Barton, L. A. (1991). *The effects of low-ability group placement on first-graders (ability grouping).* Texas A&M University: Doctoral dissertation.

Battistich, V., Solomon, D., & Delucchio, K. (1993). Interaction processes and student outcomes in cooperative learning groups. *Elementary School Journal, 94*(1), 19–32.

Beyersdorfer, J. M., & Schauer, D. (1993). All work and no play? Add play production to literacy learning. *Journal of Reading, 37*(1), 4–10.

Brinton, M. C. (1988). The social-institutional bases of gender stratification: Japan as an illustrative case. *American Journal of Sociology, 94*(2), 300–334.

Bruneau, B. J. (1992). Restructuring practice to facilitate children's literacy learning: A case study of teacher-initiated curricular change. *Teaching Education, 4*(2), 69–76.

Burr, M. Y. (1931). *A study of homogeneous grouping*. New York: Teachers College Press.

Chall, J. S., & Squire, J. R. (1991). The publishing industry and textbooks. In R. Barr, M. Kamil, P. Mosenthal, & P. D. Pearson (Eds.), *Handbook of reading research* (Vol. 2, pp. 120–146). New York: Longman.

Clay, M. (1985). *The patterning of complex behavior*. Portsmouth, NH: Heinemann.

Collins, J. (1986). Differential treatment in reading instruction. In J. Cook-Gumperz (Ed.), *The social construction of literacy* (pp. 117–137). Cambridge: Cambridge University Press.

Cummings, W. K. (1980). *Education and equality in Japan*. Princeton, NJ: Princeton University Press.

Cunningham, P. M. (1991). Making seatwork work. *Reading Horizons, 31*(4), 286–298.

Cunningham, P. M., Hall, D. P., & Defee, M. (1991). Non-ability grouped, multilevel instruction: A year in a first-grade classroom. *The Reading Teacher, 44*(8), 566–571.

Dahl, K. L. (1993). Children's spontaneous utterances during early reading and writing instruction in whole-language classrooms. *Journal of Reading Behavior, 25*(3), 279–294.

Dooley, C. (1993). The challenge: Meeting the needs of gifted readers. *The Reading Teacher, 45*(7), 546–551.

Dreeben, R., & Barr, R. (1988). The formation and instruction of ability groups. *American Journal of Education, 97,* 34–61.

Duffy, G. G. (1993). Rethinking strategy instruction: Four teachers' development and their low achievers' understandings. *Elementary School Journal, 93*(3), 231–247.

Eash, M. J. (1961). Grouping: What have we learned? *Educational Leadership, 18,* 429–434.

Eldredge, L. (1991). An experiment with a modified whole language approach in first-grade classrooms. *Reading Research and Instruction, 30*(3), 21–38.

Eldredge, J. L., & Butterfield, D. (1984). *Sacred cows make good hamburger: A report on a reading research project titled "Testing the Sacred Cows in Reading"* (ERIC Document Reproduction Service No. ED 255 861).

Eldredge, J. L., & Butterfield, D. (1986). Alternatives to traditional reading instruction. *The Reading Teacher, 40,* 32–37.

Esposito, D. (1973). Homogeneous and heterogeneous ability grouping: Principal findings and implications for evaluating and designing more effective educational environments. *Review of Educational Research, 43,* 163–179.

Findley, W., & Bryan, M. C. (1971). *Ability grouping: 1970—II: The impact of ability grouping on school achievement, affective development, ethnic separation, and socioeconomic separation*. Athens: University of Georgia, Center for Educational Improvement. (ERIC Document Reproduction Service No. ED 048 382)

Flood, J., Lapp, D., Flood, S., & Nagel, G. (1992). Am I allowed to group? Using flexible patterns for effective instruction. *The Reading Teacher, 45*(8), 608–616.

Freepon, P. A. (1991). Children's concepts of the nature and purpose of reading in different instructional settings. *Journal of Reading Behavior, 23*(2), 139–163.

Hart, A. H. (1990). *Cultural change and conservation: The implementation of the Paideia Proposal in four schools*. University of North Carolina, Greensboro: Doctoral dissertation.

Goodlad, J. I. (1984). *A place called school*. New York: McGraw-Hill.

Harrison, A. E. (1989). *Ability grouping: Practices and perspectives of elementary school teachers.* University of Massachusetts: Doctoral Dissertation.

Hartill, R. M. (1936). *Homogeneous grouping.* New York: Teachers College Press.

Hiebert, E. H. (1983). An examination of ability grouping for reading instruction. *Reading Research Quarterly, 18,* 231–255.

Hiebert, E. H. (1991). Becoming literate in whole language classrooms: Evidence and adaptions. Research address presented at the Thirty-sixth Annual Convention of the International Reading Association, Las Vegas, NV.

Hiebert, E. H., Colt, J. M., Catto, S. L., & Gury, E. C. (1992). Reading and writing of first-grade students in a restructured Chapter 1 program. *American Educational Research Journal, 29*(3), 545–572.

Homan, S. P., Hines, C. V., & Kromrey, J. D. (1993). An investigation of varying reading level placement on reading achievement of Chapter 1 student. *Reading Research and Instruction, 33*(1), 29–38.

Hoyt, L. (1992). Many ways of knowing: Using drama, oral interactions, and the visual arts to enhance reading comprehension. *The Reading Teacher, 45*(8), 580–584.

Hunter, D. (1978). Student on-task behavior during second grade reading group meetings (Doctoral dissertation, University of Missouri–Columbia, 1978). *Dissertation Abstracts International, 39,* 4838A.

Johnson, K. E. (1992). The relationship between teachers' beliefs and practices during literacy instruction for non-native speakers of English. *Journal of Reading Behavior, 24*(1), 83–108.

Juel, C. (1988). Learning to read and write: A longitudinal study of fifty-four children from first through fourth grades. *Journal of Educational Psychology, 80,* 437–447.

Kameenui, E. J. (1993). Diverse learners and the tyranny of time: Don't fix blame; fix the leaky roof. *The Reading Teacher, 45*(5), 376–383.

Keegan, S., & Shrake, K. (1991). Literature study groups: An alternative to ability grouping. *The Reading Teacher, 44*(8), 542–547.

Klesius, J. P., Griffith, P. L., & Zielonka, P. (1991). A whole language and traditional instruction comparison: Overall effectiveness and development of the alphabetic principle. *Reading Research and Instruction, 30*(2), 47–61.

Kulik, C. C., & Kulik, J. A. (1982). The relationship between self and achievement/performance measures. *American Educational Research Journal, 19,* 415–428.

Lim, H. L., & Watson, D. J. (1993). Whole language content classes for second-language learners. *The Reading Teacher, 45*(5), 384–393.

Mason, J. M., Anderson, R. C., Omura, A., Uchida, N., & Imai, M. (1989). Learning to read in Japan. *Journal of Curriculum Studies, 21,* 389–407.

Miller, W. S., & Otto, J. (1930). Analysis of experimental studies in homogeneous grouping. *Journal of Educational Research, 21,* 95–102.

Morrow, L. (1992). The impact of a literature-based program on literacy achievement, use of literature, and attitudes of children from minority backgrounds. *Reading Research Quarterly, 27*(3), 250–275.

Noland, T. K. (1985). *The effects of ability grouping: A meta-analysis of research findings.* Unpublished doctoral dissertation, University of Colorado, Boulder.

Oldfather, P. (1993). What students say about motivating experiences in a whole language classroom. *The Reading Teacher, 46*(8), 672–681.

Otto, H. J. (1932). *Current practices in the organization of elementary schools.* Evanston, IL: Northwestern University, School of Education.

Pace, G. (1992). Stories of teacher-initiated change from traditional to whole-language literacy instruction. *Elementary School Journal, 92*(4), 461–476.

Pardo, L. S., & Raphael, T. E. (1991). Classroom organization for instruction in content areas. *The Reading Teacher, 44*(8), 556–565.

Pikulski, J. H. (1991, June). Grouping for literacy instruction: A need for thoughtful reconsideration. *Florida Reading Quarterly,* pp. 7–12.

Pinnell, G. (1989). Success of children at risk in a program that combines writing and reading. In J. Mason (Ed.), *Reading and writing connections.* Needham Heights: Allyn and Bacon.

Purcell-Gates, V., & Dahl, K. L. (1991). Low-SES children's success and failure at early literacy learning in skills-based classrooms. *Journal of Reading Behavior, 23*(1), 1–34.

Rohlen, T. P. (1983). *Japan's high schools.* Berkeley: University of California Press.

Rosenholtz, S. J., & Cohen, E. G. (1983). Back to basics and the desegregated school. *Elementary School Journal, 83,* 515–527.

Scala, M. A. (1993). What whole language in the mainstream means for children with learning disabilities. *The Reading Teacher, 47*(3), 222–229.

Schafer, W. E., & Olexa, C. (1971). *Tracking and opportunity.* Scranton, PA: Chandler.

Slavin, R. E. (1983). *Cooperative learning.* New York: Longman.

Slavin, R. E. (1987). Ability grouping: A best-evidence synthesis. *Review of Educational Research, 57,* 293–336.

Smith, N. B. (1965). *American reading instruction.* Newark, DE: International Reading Association.

Stevens, R. J., Madden, N. A., Slavin, R. E., & Farnish, A. M. (1987). Cooperative integrated reading and composition: Two field experiments. *Reading Research Quarterly, 12,* 433–454.

Stevenson, H. W., & Lee, S. (1990). Contexts of achievement. *Monographs of the Society for Research in Child Development, Serial No. 221, 55*(1–2).

Stevenson, H. W., Lee, S. Y., Stigler, J. W., Kitamura, S., Kimura, S., & Kato, T. (1988). Learning to read Japanese. In H. W. Stevenson, H. Azuma, & K. Hakuta (Eds.), *Child development and education in Japan.* New York: Freeman.

Stevenson, H. W., & Stigler, J. W. (1992). *The learning gap.* New York: Summit Books.

Stice, C. F., & Bertrand, J. E. (1992). What's going on here? A qualitative examination of grouping patterns in an exemplary whole language classroom. *Reading Horizons, 32*(5), 383–393.

Stigler, J. W., & Stevenson, H. W. (1991). How Asian teachers polish each lesson to perfection. *American Educator, 15*(1), 12–20, 43–47.

Swift, K. (1993). Try Reading Workshop in your classroom. *The Reading Teacher, 46*(5), 366–371.

Taylor, B. M., Short, R. A., Frye, B. J., & Shearer, B. A. (1992). Classroom teachers prevent reading failure among low-achieving first-grade students. *The Reading Teacher, 45*(8), 592–597.

Tyack, D. (1974). *The one best system.* Cambridge, MA: Harvard University Press.

Uhry, J. K., & Shepherd, M. J. (1993). Segmentation/spelling instruction as part of a first-grade program: Effects on several measures of reading. *Reading Research Quarterly, 28*(3), 218–233.

Venezky, R. L. (1988). *The American reading script and its nineteenth century origins.*

The First Marilyn Sadow Memorial Lecture, Department of Education, University of Chicago, Chicago.

Wasik, B. A., & Slavin, R. E. (1993). Preventing early reading failure with one-to-one tutoring: A review of five programs. *Reading Research Quarterly, 28*(2), 179–200.

Weinstein, R. S. (1976). Reading group membership in first grade: Teacher behaviors and pupil experience over time. *Journal of Educational Psychology, 68*, 103–116.

West, P. (1933). *A study of ability grouping in the elementary school.* New York: Teachers College, Columbia University.

Whipple, G. M. (1936). *The grouping of pupils.* Thirty-fifth Yearbook of the National Society for the Study of Education (Part 1). Chicago: University of Chicago Press.

White, M. (1987). *The Japanese educational challenge.* New York: Free Press.

▶ 2

Keeping Flexible Groups Flexible: Grouping Options

**MARGUERITE C. RADENCICH,
LYN J. McKAY, and
JEANNE R. PARATORE**

Grouping students for the teaching of reading and language arts is one of the most challenging tasks a teacher faces. Teachers who adjust to meet the needs of all students manipulate grouping options to maximize learning.

Teachers are well aware of the lack of flexibility and the questionable effects of the traditional three-block plan of ability grouping for students in low groups, such as less wait time, lower levels of questions asked, and slower pacing (see Chapter 1). Sometimes the temptation is to search for a clear alternative to the three-block plan. Unfortunately, it is not so simple. No single-faceted plan, whether it is peer tutoring, small groups for repeated reading practice, needs-based groups, or whole-class instruction, will meet the requirements of every student. As we move toward alternative grouping plans, we must be careful to avoid the rigidity that characterizes traditional ability grouping and offer students dynamic and flexible opportunities responsive to curricular goals and individual needs.

In this chapter we provide several grouping options along with some management suggestions. The grouping options are categorized as whole class, teacher-facilitated needs-based groups, cooperative groups, pairs, and individual teaching and learning. To plan for effective integration of grouping options, it is helpful to consider the strengths and weaknesses of each. The options that follow should be viewed as ad hoc groups, formed and dissolved according to need—hence, the name "flexible grouping." The use of these grouping options may apply not only to the reading/language arts period, but also to instruction in the content areas (Pardo & Raphael, 1991). Figure 2-1 suggests possible grouping options related to a list of typical classroom activities. Suggestions in the figure are explained throughout this chapter.

FIGURE 2-1   Matching of Activities to Grouping Options

	Grouping Options*				
Activities	Whole Class	Small Needs-Based Groups (Teacher-Facilitated)	Cooperative Groups	Pairs	Individuals
Teacher read-aloud	X	X			
Demonstrations/ modeling	X	X			
Repeated readings Choral/echo	X	X			
Readers'/Story Theater	X	X			
With taped story			X		X
"Mumble" reading					X
Buddy reading				X	
Second-tier guided reading for emergent and struggling readers		X			
Journals	X			X	X
Self-selected reading			X	X	X
Projects	X		X	X	X
Writing process Conferencing				X	X
Mini-lessons	X	X			
Author's chair	X		X		
Status-of-the-class (Atwell, 1987)	X				
Learning centers			X	X	X
"Early bird"		X			

*Grouping options not limited to those suggested.

WHOLE-CLASS INSTRUCTION

Whole-class instruction can meet several instructional goals, including: (a) introduction of new ideas and concepts, (b) review of recently taught skills or strategies, (c) development of a cross-curricular theme, (d) development of a common experience from which group discussion can emerge, and (e) direction for writing through Atwell's (1987) status-of-the-class meetings. As a result of the shared experience, whole-class instruction effectively puts children in touch with the social nature of reading while safety-netting the risks associated with this learning (Reutzel & Cooter, 1992).

With regard to specific literacy goals, whole-class instruction can accomplish several purposes. For example, to begin the reading assignment, whole-class grouping can be used for introducing new vocabulary; discussing background knowledge; and teacher modeling through reading aloud, making predictions, setting purposes for reading, and providing an audience, such as a student who reads to classmates through author's chair. After reading, the whole class can discuss, analyze, and extend the selection. These are all tasks that can be accomplished successfully by children across a range of performance levels. Whole-class organization can also be used for storytelling, dramatizing stories, sharing Big Books, sharing writing pieces, holding sustained silent reading and writing time, and creating language experience charts (Reutzel & Cooter, 1992). Whole-class instruction is most effective when successful completion of the task is possible without decoding fluency and when there is opportunity for discussion. Teachers report multi-ability groups generally create livelier, more interesting discussions.

Beyond literacy learning, whole-class instruction may yield positive benefits related to students' self-esteem. Students who view themselves as low achievers often develop more positive self-images when they have the opportunity to interact with their higher performing peers. Conversely, students who see themselves as "tops" can learn to appreciate the contributions of others.

Although there are many advantages to whole-class instruction, there are also disadvantages. Attention to individual needs is minimal; individual students may be less likely to participate; and instruction tends to be teacher- rather than student-centered, with less pupil/pupil interaction. Thus, overuse of whole-class instruction may prevent attainment of some important literacy goals. Particularly, it is difficult for teachers who rely too heavily on whole-group instruction to be good kidwatchers (Goodman, 1991): recognizing what each child can and can not do, and knowing which child is ready for a nudge and which child is not. Further, even if teachers were to observe specific needs, the whole-class framework simply does not allow teachers to direct a lesson to some students and not to others.

So, it is critical that whole-class teaching not take up the bulk of instructional time. "One big reading group" is not the idea. Rather, whole-class instruction should represent only one piece of the grouping puzzle. Its usefulness grows out of effective combination with other grouping options that better address individual needs.

In summary, whole-class instruction is particularly beneficial when when it meets the following goals:

- Developing background knowledge and interest in preparation for reading and writing
- Establishing meaning by teacher read-aloud of part or all of a text
- Building a common experience such as introduction to a cross-curricular theme
- Modeling the reading/writing process
- Reviewing or reminding students of previously taught skills or strategies
- Developing understanding of a text through postreading discussion

TEACHER-FACILITATED NEEDS-BASED GROUPS

Whereas whole-class instruction is designed specifically to create a shared experience, teacher-facilitated needs-based groups are intended to address diverse learning needs. Needs-based groups are based on Vygotsky's (1978) notion of scaffolding, where meeting students' needs is not so much a matter of placing them in materials at a given level as of providing the scaffolding or instructional support necessary to help them achieve *beyond* that level. This notion has led teachers and researchers to explore ways of meeting students' needs by changing the way teachers teach reading rather than by changing the material assigned (Paratore, 1991).

Teacher-facilitated needs-based groups are particularly beneficial when:

- A few individuals need additional instruction on an ad hoc basis in areas determined by teacher observation, student request, and/or testing
- Students with special needs or emergent readers require frequent, even daily, extra help
- Higher performing students need some direction or explanation in preparation for a cooperative or independent learning project

Needs-based groups may be interpreted by some to be to be traditional ability groups. We prefer to refer to them as "performance" rather than "ability" groups because the issue really is performance rather than an innate ability. These performance groups are more flexible than traditional ability groups, with students moving among different group types (e.g., skills, need, interest), rather than being restricted only to a performance group with other students at similar reading levels.

Needs-based groups are most often formed by the teacher, particularly early in the school year. Students are often able to make their own decisions, however, about the groups they wish to join. For example, in a school where one of the authors has taught, students routinely choose whether to work individually or in pairs, or whether to join the teacher in an extra help group.

Although needs-based groups are often thought of as remedial or extra help groups, it is important to emphasize that such groups may be intended to meet the special needs of higher as well as lower performing students. Research supports the need of higher achievers to work together at times (Johnson & Johnson, 1992). In a meta-analysis of studies on ability grouping, Kulik and Kulik (1992) found that flexible grouping, combined with appropriate, differentiated instruction, led to academic gains for highly able students. Dooley (1993), however, reports that surveys of teachers and observations of gifted and average students reveal little differentiation in heterogeneous classrooms.

High achievers can benefit from curriculum compacting (Renzulli, 1977), a systematic process through which proficiency in the basic curriculum is assured, instructional pacing is appropriate, and time is made available for enrichment and acceleration. Thus, high achievers might participate in initial instruction as necessary, but may then proceed to extend class reading. For example, they may read an entire book when the basal includes only a chapter, or perform in-depth explorations of thematic units or personal interests. High achievers could also be given alternative assignments to replace routine practices (e.g., teacher read-alouds of a common selection) that are unlikely to benefit them. As is true for the special needs of any type of student, modifications for high achievers should encompass both content and process.

Needs-based groups may occur before, during, or after reading a selection, based on the instruction to be provided. Sometimes they are skill/ strategy groups. For example, comprehension-building activities that occur after students read might well focus on clarifying ideas and events, or confirming predictions. Specific activities might help students understand particular parts of the selection, focus on the author's main ideas, or summarize the selection's major events.

Teachers might conduct mini-lessons (Atwell, 1987) based on their own observations, a formal curriculum guide, lessons in a basal, assessment information, or student request. These mini-lessons could be used to reinforce the strategy for those students who need additional instruction, or extend the strategy to more advanced applications (Strickland, 1992).

One risk of needs-based groups is the tendency for a few children to become permanent members. One way to maintain heterogeneity is to in-clude visitors to the group. The visiting, or rotating, members benefit in different ways. For example, a shy child may join to learn to be more assertive or questioning in the group; another child may join strictly on the basis of interest; another may join to learn more about collaboration. One such plan is Cunningham and Allington's (1993) after-lunch bunch, a small group that meets for fifteen minutes to read easy books "just for fun." The membership changes daily, with the less proficient readers as frequent, but not every day, members. Every child is included during the week, the best readers only once each week. Keeping performance groups heterogeneous and using them as only one selection in a menu of grouping options helps avoid some of the problems common with traditional ability groups.

Finally, in almost every classroom, teachers have at least one or two students for whom no amount of stretching results in successful reading of grade-appropriate text. Teachers know they must *teach* these students to read, not just allow them to listen and respond to grade-appropriate text. For such students, many teachers have implemented a "two-tier" plan similar to the multilevel instruction described by Cunningham in Chapter 7.

TWO-TIERED INSTRUCTION

Pull from top of tube
with grade-level materials

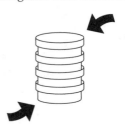

Push bottom of tube
with comfort-level materials

In one tier, students may interact with the grade-appropriate text(s)—listening to a read-aloud, learning concepts with classmates, contributing to story discussion, and writing in response. This enables them to maintain "citizenship" in the classroom community. In addition, however, they receive regular instruction and practice in easier texts, and on specific strategies and skills. A useful metaphor is that of a child stuck in a tube (S. Fields, personal communication, March 1, 1993). While you pull from the top with grade-level material, you must also push from the bottom, with comfort-level text. The comfort-level text can be predictable language books that children "zoom through with joyous familiarity" (Bill Martin in Cullinan, Greene, & Jaggar, 1990, p. 753). It may come from general trade books (individual titles available from any bookstore, and not written specifically for school curricula) and/or student-authored books. Use of lower level basals as easy reading is not recommended because of the possible negative impact on the child's self-esteem and motivation. If the class is reading from a single selection, it is helpful if the easier-tier material is thematically or otherwise related to it.

The use of an easier set of materials is particularly necessary for emergent readers. Routman (1991), for example, recommends that, at the beginning of first grade, teachers meet students in homogeneous groups as part of their instruction to help students move through books of gradually decreasing levels of predictability. Fields (S. Fields, personal communication, March 1, 1993) provides a strategy for using predictable books with homogeneous groups when multiple copies are not available. The teacher reads a few different titles and provides some guided reading instruction to the group of less proficient readers. Then, pairs of students become custodians of one of the books, which they read to each other. The teacher might package each book in a ziplock bag that also includes sight words for the pair to study. See Cunningham (1991) and Cunningham and Hall (1991) for examples of successful use of multilevel non-ability-grouped instruction with low achieving first graders.

When scheduling time for a second tier of instruction for low achievers, teachers may wish to excuse students from other assignments. These might include selection follow-ups too difficult for students significantly below level, even if completed in cooperative groups.

Following are examples of before-, during-, and after-reading strategies and practices that are particularly suited to small groups.

Teacher-Assisted Before-Reading Activities

Teacher-assisted before-reading activities can make the language and concepts more familiar through a read-aloud; make vocabulary more automatic through previewing, explicit instruction, and practice; or make events and their relationships more comprehensible through prereading discussion.

One widely used practice is the formation of an "early bird" group. This needs-based group may meet a day or two before the rest of the class begins the common selection. During this time, members may participate in a read-aloud and initial discussion and practice of vocabulary essential to reading and understanding the selection. This group might be led by the classroom teacher, a special teacher (e.g., Special Education, Chapter 1), or a volunteer or aide. "Early bird" grouping represents a way of being proactive—intervening to prevent, rather than to remediate, failure. The result: Students who often struggle to keep up may now actually outshine their otherwise higher performing peers. Teachers who try early bird grouping enthusiastically tell us, "*It works!*"

Teacher-Assisted During-Reading Activities

Teachers typically conduct the first reading in different ways depending on the nature of the group. If most students can read the selection alone, but a few cannot, the teacher might conduct a "whisper club" (S. Fields, personal communication, March 1, 1993), reading a class selection to a group of less-proficient readers while others read it to themselves. One teacher adapted this by having strong readers do the whispering. If most students cannot read the selection alone, the teacher might read it to the group while higher achievers use earphones at a computer or listening-station activity, work in a quiet part of the room, or go to the school library.

Teacher-Assisted After-Reading Activities

Teacher-assisted activities for needs-based groups can also occur after reading. Among the most useful practices is repeated readings of passages about one hundred words long with an emphasis on speed more than accuracy (Samuels, Schermer, & Reinking, 1992). Use of repeated readings has received extensive support in the professional literature. A wide range of studies (Chomsky, 1978; Koskinen & Blum, 1984; McGuinan, 1968; O'Shea, Sindelar, & O'Shea, 1985; Samuels, 1979; Spring, Blunden, & Gatheral, 1981) indicates that even one rereading can increase both fluency and comprehension. Additional readings increase them further. Three to five practice readings appear to be optimal for the development of fluency, even with below-average readers.

Teachers using repeated readings should provide multiple purposes for the reading. These can include confirming predictions; identifying the most exciting, scariest, or funniest parts of a book; or developing expression in reading dialogue, perhaps during a play or puppet production of the text (Strickland, 1992).

Teachers may read selections aloud to a class or group, perhaps tape-recording themselves in the process to provide rereading material for a listening center. Other alternatives include teachers dividing up selections to record, or asking high performing readers to do the recording. Other repeated reading activities that can be teacher-directed and are easy to use as initial rereadings include:

- Various forms of choral reading
- Echo reading, with the length of the chunks progressing throughout the year, perhaps from phrases to sentences or sentence clusters (Morris & Nelson, 1992)
- Assigning groups to each character in story theater and readers' theater

Types of rereadings that require less teacher direction and invite more pupil interaction include:

- Buddy or partner reading (see Pairs, p. 35) of the selection, or of a portion or adaptation of the selection (i.e., first and last page, one page or one paragraph, a story summary, or a predictable version of the story)
- Assigning individual parts for story or readers' theater

Finally, successful use of small needs-based groups requires some system for classroom management. The timeworn idea of learning centers can be dusted off and reconceptualized a bit to help teachers manage small groups simultaneously, while offering some extra help and other challenging activities. Centers can be made up of materials brought by teachers and students alike. Third-grade teacher Caryl Crowell (1991) includes materials in the students' native languages in the centers in her multilanguage classroom. Included in thematic or more general centers for early readers can be follow-ups to predictable books:

- Sentence strips or word cards to sequence
- Materials for students to use in making reproductions (copies) of predictable books in varied formats such as accordion books, ziplock-bag books, or Big Books
- Frames for students to use in writing their own innovations (_____ , _____ , *who do you see? I see* _____ *looking at me.*)
- Computer use in completing story reproductions and innovations
- Materials for use in dramatizing the selections or innovations

Teachers in classrooms where space is limited might pair up with an adjoining classroom. One alternative is to use manila envelopes, shoe boxes, or milk crates to house center activities, which are then taken to the students' seats.

COOPERATIVE GROUPS

Of all grouping options, cooperative grouping may represent the best opportunity for every student to contribute to the group. As one second-grade teacher commented, "The children like cooperative grouping because they get to work with different students in their class. It takes the pressure off because everybody has something to add to the group."

Research (Slavin, 1991) indicates children in cooperative-learning groups consistently show increased achievement, self-concept, and social skills. Cooperative groups may provide a forum for sharing predictions and ideas, or for discussing and responding to one or more selections. Members of cooperative groups are interdependent. All group members have responsibilities for group and individual learning. Cooperative groups may be used before or after reading.

Cooperative groups are typically formed with three to six students, but most often three to four. Tasks may be assigned, or students may select among several options. Tasks frequently culminate in a written group product. Examples include: comparing predictions made prior to reading and actual story events, describing character traits and their impact on the story, listing predictions, summarizing a selection, or comparing a selection with one read previously. Tasks are structured so face-to-face interaction among group members is possible, with both interdependence among members (sink or swim together) and individual accountability (Johnson, Johnson, & Holubec, 1990).

Possible cooperative groups include the following:

- Interest groups that work on theme projects
- Literature response groups where groups of students each read and discuss a different title
- Computer work groups where rotating roles can be keyboard operator, monitor, and checker
- Story-retelling groups where each group member retells a story read to the group and fields comments

Appropriate procedures for cooperative grouping may vary from culture to culture. Vogt, Jordan, and Tharp (1987) report high levels of peer interaction and helping among heterogeneous groups of native Hawaiian students. However, when Vogt et al. attempted to use these same arrangements with Navajo students, they found resistance. Better success came when restricting cooperative learning to single-sex groups, because of the distinct and separate gender roles in Navajo culture. Au (1993) also contrasts native Hawaiian interactions, where students persist in efforts to help peers even when the targeted students initially refuse assistance, with Yup'ik Eskimo students, where help is more subtle and less obviously intrusive.

Cooperative learning is a grouping practice that has received abundant support from researchers and teachers. Most agree, however, it requires thoughtful planning and execution. Johnson, Johnson, and Holubec's *Circles of Learning* (1990) is an excellent source for more general information on cooperative learning. Keegan and Shrake (1991) provide specifics about using cooperative learning to support literacy learning.

PAIRS

Cooperative pairs are perhaps the easiest form of cooperative grouping to manage. Pairs allow both for "less negotiation and more opportunity to construct" (Berghoff & Egawa, 1991). Pairs can be ideal for the following literacy tasks:

- Finding and recording information
- Planning, co-authoring, revising, and drafting writing
- Interviewing a partner and responding to the book the partner has read
- Testing each other on material each has studied
- Listing predictions in preparation for reading
- Completing everyday tasks, which might otherwise have been independent seatwork
- Solving problems

Following are a number of paired-learning variations.

━━➤ 1. Peer Tutoring.   Peer turoring involves a more proficient student tutoring a less proficient student, either within the classroom or across grade levels. The responsibility of peer tutors is generally to reinforce previous teaching. This grouping option provides opportunities for practice and benefits both tutors and tutees in achievement, self-concept, social relationships, and attitudes toward reading (Cohen, Kulik, & Kulik, 1982; Topping, 1989). Topping (1989) provides several suggestions that promote effective implementation of peer tutoring. He emphasizes: (a) training and modeling for tutors increases the procedure's effectiveness; (b) training should include appropriate ways of correcting, giving praise, and stimulating learning; and (c) the differential in proficiency between the students should allow the tutor to provide an adequate model of competency.

━━➤ 2. Reciprocal Teaching.   One of the most well-known and most effective peer-tutoring strategies for use with pairs or small groups is reciprocal teaching (Palincsar & Brown, 1984; Palincsar, Brown, & Martin, 1987). Reciprocal teaching strategies include clarifying, summarizing, questioning, and predicting, allowing lower performing students to reread and respond to small segments of text with more able students who model, support, and extend their understanding. Reciprocal teaching can be used before, during, and after reading.

━━➤ 3. Partner Reading.   Another activity that can, but need not, be a form of peer tutoring is partner or buddy reading. Partner reading provides practice that promotes fluency in word recognition and comprehension. The listener can enhance comprehension through discussion and questioning (Topping, 1989). Within pairs, students often alternate the reading of a selection. As one student reads, the other follows the text, assisting with unknown words as necessary. Unevenly matched partners may each be given the choice, for example, of (a) reading a paragraph or a page, (b) reading difficult parts together, or (c) following along while the partner does the reading. Making a choice can help both partners feel ownership in the activity.

One variation of buddy reading is the use of pairs where each student reads a portion of text silently, or, in some cases, orally in unison (Wood, 1987). One student acts as recaller, verbally recounting what the two had read. The buddy acts as listener and clarifier for the recaller. Paired reading effectively supports young children's reading development, especially for at-risk readers (Eldredge & Quinn, 1988).

One of two final paired activities includes reading aloud in content areas. Students take turns reading aloud to the class one or two paragraphs assigned to practice. They alternate until passages are read aloud fluently (Pardo & Raphael, 1991). In the second paired activity, Think-Pair-Share (McTighe & Lyman, 1988), students think about a high-level question, quickly discuss it in a pair, and then share their thinking with the whole group.

Paired learning can fit effectively into the classroom routine with little preparation, and can be monitored with ease. It is a useful way to stretch instructional time and provide students with practice in reading connected text.

INDIVIDUAL TEACHING AND LEARNING

While working with individuals is not strictly a form of grouping, it is addressed here because of its vital place in the overall classroom organization. Individual teaching often takes place in one-on-one conferences. These serve not only to personalize instruction and to review skills/strategies taught to large or small groups, but also to monitor the progress of individual students (Strickland, 1992). As fifth-grade teacher Debra Goodman stated: "The twenty minutes that I spent with Amanda that day were probably some of the most valuable minutes she spent in my class" (Goodman & Curry, 1991, p. 152).

As opposed to individual teaching, individual learning takes place in any grouping situation. Particularly important for individual learning are times when students set their own goals/purposes, reflect on ideas and on their progress, apply and practice skills/concepts/strategies, do self-selected reading and writing, and engage in personal creative tasks. Strategies and activities students may practice alone include journal writing, question generation, project development, and some types of repeated readings (e.g., following along with audiotaped selection, "mumble" reading, and simple rereadings). When teachers choose to use a single text with the whole class, there is a risk that some students may be "held back" or not be given enough opportunities to read and write on their own. Ample opportunities for individual practice and extension are important and should not be neglected in the effort to build more collaborative learning environments.

MANAGEMENT SUGGESTIONS

"Yes, but how do I put this all together?" is the key question. Conversations with teachers suggest that "putting it all together" can be both intimidating and difficult. Combine the ideas of several teachers and the following list of guidelines emerges:

➤ **1.** Introduce general procedures a step at a time, helping students to gradually acquire reading and writing routines. For example, one second-grade teacher outlines her procedures as follows: (paraphrased)

On the first day of school, we introduced a song from a chart, sang it together, and read a few predictable books. We showed students where these books would be kept, in case they wanted to read them on their own when making choices later. Then we began to introduce writing workshop to the whole group. Everyone received a portfolio and listed possible ideas they could write about. Everyone started their first written piece, and, when they wrote all they wanted to, they decided to read, individually or in pairs, the song or the books.

On the next day, we continued introducing more elements of writing workshop, while adding a few new easy books to the growing collection and singing the songs. We introduced something new every few days. Especially when we introduced something that was quite different, we would all do it together before it became one of a growing list of choices. We listed the choices on a large chart as we introduced them so that, when we were ready for the children to make their own choices, we reviewed the options from the chart. Our time together developed a very regular structure, and we soon did not need to refer to the chart (Jacobson, 1991).

━━▶ **2.** If students are expected to move through several centers, provide a system that helps children to make appropriate choices. For example, a fifth-grade teacher makes a Velcro board listing optional centers and activities on the left, with as many spaces to the right as the number of students who can work on an option at one time. Students attach a construction paper shape with Velcro backing as they go to an activity of their choice. Activities may take place throughout the day and are usually untimed. The activities are:

- Listening station
- Computer station
- Writing station
- Sitting on floor by classroom library
- Buddy reading with nature (outside)
- VIP chair (for reading with teacher, aide, or older/younger student)
- Teacher (one-on-one conference over work, or time to chat)
- Rainbow (electronic cards)
- Language master
- Mini filmstrip projector
- Math manipulatives
- Science/social studies

Another intermediate teacher uses a magazine rack to label activities and inserts index cards with student names in the appropriate places. A New Zealand primary teacher makes a "Things I Can Do" book with photographs of children engaged in optional activities. The book grows throughout the year. Children use the book for ideas when they have time for optional activities.

━━▶ **3.** Provide ongoing activities for children to turn to as they finish assigned work. One reading coordinator suggests having ongoing projects that allow time for meaningful activity. This also reduces the problems created when students finish before others.

Beyond these suggestions for management, you will need to devise your own grouping plan. As you read the next two chapters, consider which aspects of the individual plans may work for you and which will not. In experimenting with various grouping options to devise your own plan, you may want to follow the suggestions below:

- Closely observe and assess students to learn their strengths and weaknesses, both initially and throughout the year.
- Model to ensure that your students understand strategies and appropriate group behavior (Strickland, 1992).

- Map out a tentative plan of grouping options to try at the beginning of the year, and alternatives to add to the repertoire while exploring new combinations.
- Keep a log of experiences in matching grouping options with curricular goals and individual needs.
- Be flexible about schedules for each subject.
- Allow students to have some ownership in choices of how they will spend their time (Atwell, 1987).
- Observe and network with colleagues to support each other while trying new grouping options.
- Continually read and reread relevant professional publications.

The management plans devised by individual teachers will be unique and pliable. Mold them to meet a class's particular needs.

CONCLUDING REMARKS

In this chapter we have categorized grouping options as whole class, teacher-facilitated needs-based groups, cooperative groups, pairs, and individual teaching and learning. We see these as ad hoc groups, each with potential strengths and weaknesses. To assist teachers in forming and dissolving groups according to need, we have also provided management ideas and suggestions to consider in developing a local plan. Chapters 3 and 4 put grouping options into plans for organized literacy instruction.

REFERENCES

Atwell, N. (1987). *In the middle: Writing, reading, and learning with adolescents.* Portsmouth, NH: Heinemann.

Au, K. H. (1993). *Literacy instruction in multicultural settings.* Orlando, FL: Harcourt Brace Jovanovich.

Berghoff, B., & Egawa, K. (1991). No more "rocks": Grouping to give students control of their learning. *The Reading Teacher, 44,* 536–541.

Chomsky, C. (1978). When you still can't read in third grade: After decoding, what? In S. J. Samuels (Ed.), *What research has to say about reading instruction* (pp. 13–30). Newark, DE: International Reading Association.

Crowell, C. G. (1991). Becoming biliterate in a whole language classroom. In Y. M. Goodman, W. J. Hood, & K. S. Goodman (Eds.), *Organizing for whole language* (pp. 95–111). Portsmouth, NH: Heinemann.

Cullinan, P. M. (1991). Research directions: Multimethod, multilevel literacy instruction in first grade. *Language Arts, 68*, 578–584.

Cunningham, P. M., & Allington, R. L. (1993). *Classrooms that work—They can all read and write*. New York: HarperCollins.

Cunningham, P. M., & Hall, D. P. (1991). Non-ability-grouped, multilevel instruction: A year in a first-grade classroom. *The Reading Teacher, 44*, 566–571.

Dooley, C. (1993). The challenge: Meeting the needs of gifted readers. *The Reading Teacher, 46*, 546–551.

Eldredge, J. L., & Quinn, D. W. (1988). Increasing reading performance of low-achieving second graders with dyad reading groups. *Journal of Educational Research, 82*, 40–46.

Goodman, D., & Curry, T. K. (1991). Teaching in the real world. In Y. M. Goodman, W. J. Hood, & K. S. Goodman (Eds.), *Organizing for whole language* (pp. 137–169). Portsmouth, NH: Heinemann.

Goodman, Y. (1991). Kidwatching includes kidlistening as well. In R. S. Goodman, L. B. Bird, & Y. M. Goodman (Eds.), *Whole language catalog* (p. 208). Santa Rosa, CA: American School Publishers.

Jacobson, D. (1991). The Chapter I reading teacher enters the classroom. In Y. M. Goodman, W. J. Hood, & K. S. Goodman (Eds.), *Organizing for whole language* (pp. 316–322). Portsmouth, NH: Heinemann.

Johnson, D. W., & Johnson, R. T. (1992). What to say to advocates for the gifted. *Educational Leadership, 50*(2), 44–47.

Johnson, D. W., Johnson, R. T., & Holubec, E. (1990). *Circles of learning: Cooperation in the classroom* (3rd ed.). Edina, MN: Interaction Book Company.

Keegan, S., & Shrake, K. (1991). Literature study groups: An alternative to ability grouping. *The Reading Teacher, 44*, 542–547.

Koskinen, P. S., & Blum, I. H. (1984). Repeated oral reading and the acquisition of fluency. In J. A. Niles & L. A. Harris (Eds.), *Changing perspectives on research in reading/language processing and instruction, Thirty-third Yearbook of the National Reading Conference* (pp. 183–187). Rochester, NY: National Reading Conference.

Kulik, J. A., & Kulik, C. C. (1992). Meta-analytic findings on grouping programs. *Gifted Child Quarterly, 36*, 73–77.

McGuinan, F. J. (1968). *Experimental psychology*. Englewood Cliffs, NJ: Prentice Hall.

McTighe, J., & Lyman, F. T. (1988, April). Cueing thinking in the classroom: The promise of theory-embedded tools. *Educational Leadership, 45*, 18–24.

Morris, D., & Nelson, L. (1992). Supported oral reading with low achieving second graders. *Reading Research and Instruction, 32*(1), 49–63.

O'Shea, L. J., Sindelar, P. T., & O'Shea, D. J. (1985). The effects of repeated readings and attentional cues on reading fluency and comprehension. *Journal of Reading Behavior, 17*(2), 129–142.

Palincsar, A. S., & Brown, A. L. (1984). Reciprocal teaching of comprehension-fostering and comprehension-monitoring activities. *Cognition and Instruction, 1*(2), 117–175.

Palincsar, A. S., Brown, A. L., & Martin, S. M. (1987). Peer interaction in reading comprehension instruction. *Educational Psychologist, 22*, 231–253.

Paratore, J. R. (1991). Flexible grouping: Why and how. *The Leadership Letters—Issues and Trends in Reading and Language Arts.* Columbus, OH: Silver Burdett & Ginn.

Pardo, L. S., & Raphael, T. E. (1991). Classroom organization for instruction in content areas. *The Reading Teacher, 44,* 556–565.

Renzulli, J. S. (1977). What makes a problem real: Stalking the illusive meaning of qualitative differences in gifted education. *Gifted Child Quarterly, 26,* 147–156.

Reutzel, D. R., & Cooter, R. B. (1992). *Teaching children to read.* New York: Macmillan.

Samuels, S. J. (1979). The method of repeated readings. *The Reading Teacher, 32,* 403–408.

Samuels, S. J., Schermer, N., & Reinking, D. (1992). Reading fluency: Techniques for making decoding automatic. In S. J. Samuels & A. E. Farstrup (Eds.), *What research has to say about reading instruction* (pp. 124–144). Newark, DE: International Reading Association.

Spring, C., Blunden, D., & Gatheral, M. (1981). Effect on reading comprehension of training to automaticity in word-reading. *Perceptual and Motor Skills, 53,* 779–786.

Strickland, D. S. (1992). Organizing a literature-based reading program. In B. E. Cullinan (Ed.), *Invitation to read: More children's literature in the reading program.* Newark, DE: International Reading Association.

Topping, K. (1989). Peer tutoring and paired reading: Combining two powerful techniques. *The Reading Teacher, 42,* 488–494.

Vogt, L. A., Jordan, C., & Tharp, R. G. (1987). Explaining school failure, producing school success: Two cases. *Anthropology and Education Quarterly, 18*(4), 276–286.

Vygotsky, L. S. (1978). *Mind in society.* Cambridge, MA: Harvard University Press.

Wood, K. D. (1987). Fostering cooperative learning in middle and secondary level classrooms. *Journal of Reading, 31,* 10–18.

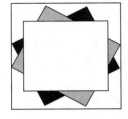

► 3

Implementing Flexible Grouping with a Common Reading Selection

**MARGUERITE C. RADENCICH, LYN J. McKAY,
JEANNE R. PARATORE, GLORIA L. PLAZA,
KAY E. LUSTGARTEN, PAT NELMS,
and PAMELA T. MOORE**

Integration and thoughtful selection of grouping options in response to students' needs is a critical component in the effective teaching of reading. Following are three flexible grouping plans, each based on the use of a common text for all students. Flexible grouping need not, however, be centered around a single selection shared by every student. Chapter 4 discusses suggestions for using flexible grouping with multiple titles.

In the first two plans in this chapter, teachers start from a specific model and then adapt it. In the third, teachers are given a more general direction and make selections in a less structured manner. Additional plans beginning with a common grade-appropriate selection include Cunningham's (Cunningham, 1991b; Cunningham & Hall, 1991) first-grade model; Wiggins's (1994) model for students close to, on, and above grade level; and Strickland's (1992) broad organizational framework.

PINELLAS COUNTY FLEXIBLE-GROUPING MODEL

Over 2,000 elementary teachers in Pinellas County, Florida's seventh largest school district, switched from traditional ability grouping to a flexible-grouping model for reading instruction during the 1990–1991 school year. Pinellas County is a metropolitan school district in the Tampa Bay Area with 84 elementary schools and 45,000 students in kindergarten through Grade 5. Preparation for the change to flexible grouping spanned a year and involved hundreds of teachers, administrators, and parents in piloting, planning, and curriculum writing.

When the teachers moved away from traditional ability grouping, they adopted a flexible-grouping model symbolized by four circles (see Figure 3-1). The essential instructional elements of the model—reading-selection instruction, writing, self-selected reading, and skill and strategy instruction—are linked by enrichment activities. The parallel placement of the circles signifies the equal importance of all four elements, taught in any order. Interrelated and interdependent, the elements frequently overlap, and teachers often integrate them.

Usually, each of the four elements is taught daily. Together, the four circle activities fill the time a teacher would have devoted in the past to meeting with ability groups, or they encompass the approximately two and one-half hours a teacher and students devote to reading and language arts.

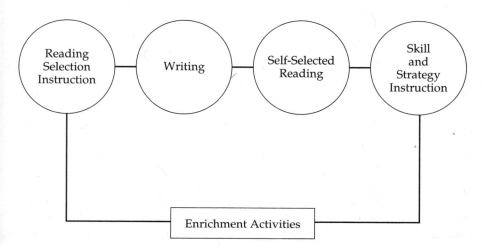

FIGURE 3-1　Pinellas County Flexible Grouping, Core-Selection Model for Teaching Reading, K–5

Source: Reprinted with permission from Pinellas County Schools.

The materials teachers use for reading include (1) a core selection, which is a grade-level basal or a paperback book with copies for all students, and (2) a wide range of supplementary paperback books, including multiple copies of predictable texts, and other information and literature reading materials. Following is a description of the model in detail.

Reading-Selection Instruction

During the reading-selection instructional time period, which occupies about one-fourth of daily reading instruction, the teacher teaches all students from a single text. In most cases, the teacher delivers instruction initially to the whole class in a shared reading setting. The teacher's primary goal is to promote understanding. A secondary goal is to teach, through modeling, a specific skill or strategy. This instruction is frequently followed by heterogeneously paired reading, cooperative group work, and/or small-group teaching. Instruction moves alternately between whole-group instruction and small-group interaction. The activities typically used in reading-selection instruction can be divided into four categories: preparing to read, reading and rereading, discussion, and skill instruction and practice. It usually takes two to three days to complete all four activities for one selection.

Preparing to Read (primarily whole class).   Preparing to read is usually a whole-class activity. The teacher begins by building background and eliciting predictions and then often reads all or part of the text aloud to students. New vocabulary is introduced through activities such as semantic mapping, and the teacher encourages students to ask questions about the selection. This activity takes about 15–20 minutes, depending on the grade level and selection.

Reading and Rereading (primarily small flexible groups).   Students break into a wide variety of grouping patterns for reading and rereading. For example, some students might read the selection independently and write in response to what they have read, some students who need extra help might meet with the teacher for a guided reading lesson, and some students might listen to the selection on audiotapes and write or draw in response to the selection. Next, all students who responded by writing or drawing might meet with the teacher while the other students meet in pairs to create a story map. The entire class might then participate in partner oral reading of the text and rereading of familiar stories. Frequently, teachers start the reading and rereading activities on one day and complete them the next day. These activities typically consume a total of about 45 minutes.

The number and kinds of groups a teacher employs are limited only by a teacher's ingenuity. Flexibility is the key. A teacher might meet with a

group working on a theme-related project while the rest of the class participates in oral reading with partners. At another time, the teacher might divide the class into three groups, one reading independently, one working
with partners writing in response to reading, and one working at centers.
The teacher circulates and intervenes as necessary.

Although students are generally grouped heterogeneously in this flexible-grouping model, there are times when grouping by ability or like needs
is necessary. For example, struggling readers might need to meet with the
teacher to participate in teacher-guided oral reading activities such as assisted reading and repeated reading. At this time, students might use easy-
to-read material, selections previously read with the whole group, or experience stories based on the core text. Emergent and early readers, too, need
an opportunity to be in needs-alike guided reading groups as they learn to
use cueing strategies and to self-monitor their reading. Both struggling readers and emergent readers participate with the class during large-group shared
reading time, working in the same text as is used to instruct the whole group.
It is during small-group guided reading sessions that they read from text
specific to their instructional needs. This pattern of instruction appears to
be particularly beneficial in the primary grades as teachers make the transition from traditional ability grouping to a more flexible-grouping model of
instruction. As well as providing needs-alike groups for struggling and
emerging readers, the teacher may call highly skilled readers together at
times to work on a cooperative writing project such as publishing student
interviews on favorite books. Whatever the purpose for grouping, groups
remain intact for only short periods of time. Small groups continually re-
group as members change.

Discussion (primarily whole class).   Discussion is primarily a whole-class
activity that follows reading and rereading. During this time, students may
confirm predictions, retell the story, summarize, and/or compare the selection to selections previously read. This activity has the advantage of allowing interaction among students at all levels. Students are encouraged to generate questions, comments, and responses. Unlike discussion in former traditional ability groups, this interaction among students, and between students and the teacher, is more student-centered. Discussion usually takes
about 15–20 minutes.

***Skill Instruction Specific to a Common Text and Practice as Needed
(whole-class and/or small flexible groups).***   The flexible-grouping core
selection model has not eliminated the need for skill instruction. This instruction may follow rather than precede the introduction and reading of a
story, and it is taught in context rather than in isolation. Emergent readers
may discuss specific decoding skills or cueing strategies as the need arises

during a guided reading lesson. The teacher may model rereading for meaning using an experience story. The teacher may introduce a skill, such as skimming for pertinent information, to the whole class. Follow-up instruction and/or practice is then accomplished in small groups based on need. These follow-up groups may be cooperative groups, heterogeneous pairs, or teacher-directed extra help groups.

Writing

Process writing is an integral part of the teaching of reading. It occupies at least one-fourth of daily reading and language arts instruction. Students may work individually, in cooperative groups, and in small teacher-directed response groups. Students keep their drafts and revisions in writing folders and publish in a variety of formats from student-bound books to audiotapes.

Writing in Response to Reading.   Writing in response to reading is an important component of the flexible-grouping model. It is as significant to the teaching of reading comprehension as it is to the teaching of writing. Students at all levels frequently write personal responses inspired by the reading or rereading of all or part of a selection. Often they write two or three responses to a single selection or part of a selection.

The initial response is the first reaction a student has upon hearing or reading a story. The teacher frequently asks, "What does this passage make you think about?" or "How does this story make you feel?" Teachers treat this first response like journal writing and often engage in a written dialogue with the student. The student's second response is a focused response to one element of the passage (e.g., character, setting, word choice, use of detail). A teacher might reread a portion of a selection that describes a character and ask, "What does this rereading make you think about?" Discussion specific to the character might follow the second writing. Following are typical examples written by a Grade 4 student after reading Christobel Mattingly's *Duck Boy.*

FIRST RESPONSE: *The story made me think about how the boy felt and what he was thinking about and it made me feel the same way the boy did.*

SECOND RESPONSE: *It made me think about what would happen if he found Lucy and what exactly he was thinking about at that time. I wondered if Lucy would die and how he would react if Lucy would have died. It made me feel like I was in the story and what I would do and think if I was the boy.*

The third response is a new student-generated topic, associated directly or indirectly with previous readings, in which students relate literature to their lives. The fourth grader who responded to *Duck Boy* wrote a story about how a friend reacted to the death of his grandfather.

Other Writing. In addition to writing in response to reading, other regularly used types of writing include journal writing, narrative writing—including both personal and fictional narrative—and project and report writing. Students have pen pals as far away as China and as close as the class down the hall. From kindergarten through Grade 5, emphasis is on purposeful, authentic writing.

Sharing. Students share unfinished pieces of writing as well as finished work, and they share frequently. They share in small groups and with the whole class. Each time, the student follows his or her reading with two questions: "What do you like about my story?" and "Do you have any questions?" The answers to these questions give the writer positive reinforcement and provide direction for revision. Sometimes the teacher helps students see the similarities and differences between their own work and the work of other authors.

Self-Selected Reading

During self-selected reading, which occupies about one-quarter of daily reading instruction time, students read silently in materials on their independent or instructional levels. Students are encouraged to choose selections of interest to them. The sports section of the local newspaper is just as acceptable as *Little House on the Prairie.* When students have difficulty finding materials of interest at their reading levels, teachers guide them.

What Does the Teacher Do During Self-Selected Reading? In the past, teachers frequently read along with their students during sustained silent reading time. Although such modeling is still considered important, teachers will just as often interact with students during self-selected reading time. Some teachers conduct individual or group book chats. Others circulate and conference with students. Some call up individual students to read orally. Some meet with a small group for activities such as assisted reading, echo reading, and/or the rereading of familiar selections. Some may meet with a small heterogeneous group to discuss the elements of plot, character, or setting in the students' various selections.

Sharing. Students talk to one another daily about what they read. They do not wait until they finish a selection to share. Sharing causes students to summarize what they have read, continually exposes other students to good literature, and promotes oral language development and critical thinking skills.

Although sharing occurs frequently throughout the day, teachers often set aside a specific sharing time each day that students can count on. Teachers group students in small cooperative groups or pairs for about 5–10 minutes, often just before dismissal. Sometimes students simply turn their chairs and briefly tell what they have read that day. One teacher calls this time "popcorn sharing" to encourage students to be brief and allow each person a turn. Some teachers use timers.

General Skill and Strategy Instruction

As often as possible, skill and strategy instruction is given within the context of what the students are reading and writing. Although this instruction sometimes occurs during individual conferences and in small groups, there are some skills and strategies teachers find can be practiced successfully with the total class. Some teachers, for example, may conduct a whole-class manipulative phonics activity such as *Making Words* or a whole-class sight word activity such as *Word Wall* (Cunningham, 1991a; see also Chapter 7). These activities require students to manipulate individual letters to make words of varying lengths, or practice writing selected sight words that are added to a list posted on a classroom wall each week. Other teachers may teach the whole class the strategy of summarizing. Modeling cueing strategies for emergent and early readers using Big Books with predictable text is another whole-group activity that teachers have found successful. Following whole-group instruction, teachers sometimes divide the class into small groups for cooperative or teacher-directed practice.

Teachers have found they must be careful not to sacrifice self-selected reading time and writing time for skill instruction. Skill and strategy instruction, both small-group and whole-class, makes up no more than one-quarter of the time devoted to the teaching of reading. The typical basal reader contains more skills lessons than can be taught in the course of one school year without infringing on the time needed for more critical reading activities. Teachers must be selective to ensure a balance of shared, guided, and independent reading and writing activities for all students.

After Two Years of Using Flexible Grouping

The four circle flexible-grouping model of instruction has served as a transition to more flexible-grouping practices in Pinellas County. As teachers become more comfortable with managing groups, the four circles of instruction are becoming more integrated, and some teachers are moving away from a core selection except during shared or whole-group instruction. More small-group guided reading is occurring with increased professional development, especially in the primary grades. Literacy circles (heterogeneous groups of four or five students who discuss trade books they are reading) are emerging, especially in the intermediate grades. The four circle flexible-grouping model of teaching reading represents a good beginning.

Following is one school's adaptation of the Pinellas County flexible-grouping plan.

Sample Elementary Flexible-Grouping Schedule
Pinellas County, Florida
January of Grade 1

This schedule is a modification of a two-and-three-quarter-hour schedule developed by a group of Grade 1 teachers in Pinellas County, Florida. Subjects such as art, music, physical education, and Chapter 1 pull-out programs have been omitted. The teachers generally organize their reading and writing instruction in the order presented in this schedule with various pull-out subjects interspersed.

Day 1

45 minutes	*Self-Selected Reading and Writing (all students)*
	Teacher-directed group (extra help group; guided reading)—20 minutes
	Reread yesterday's story
	Practice words (segmenting and blending)
	Write a group sentence (guided writing)
	Read a new story
	Teacher-directed group (mixed ability)—20 minutes
	Share reading (as a literature circle with teacher as facilitator)
	Share writing in response to reading
15 minutes	*Preparing to Read (whole class)*
	Background, predicting, read aloud, and/or vocabulary
15 minutes	*Reading and Rereading (small groups)*
	Teacher-directed group (a needs-alike group; guided reading)
	Independent readers (read and write in response)
	Listening center group (listen and write/draw; may be extra help group that met earlier in the day)
15 minutes	*Vocabulary Practice (partners and small groups)*
	Teacher-directed group (independent readers and listening center students)
	Share writing and drawing
	Discuss vocabulary

(Continued)

Sample Elementary Flexible-Grouping Schedule
Pinellas County, Florida
January of Grade 1 (Continued)

Partner vocabulary practice (students who were in the needs-alike guided reading group)

15 minutes   *Phonics Instruction (whole class)*
Pat Cunningham's "Making Words"

30 minutes   *Centers*

30 minutes   *Handwriting/Teacher Read-Aloud*

Day 2

25 minutes   *Self-Selected Reading (all students)*
Teacher-directed group (extra help group)—15 minutes
Reread yesterday's story
Practice words (segmenting and blending)
Write a group sentence
Read a new story

Book chats (two or three individual student chats) or guided reading needs-alike group

25 minutes   *Writing [whole-class (shared) and individual (guided) conferences]*

15 minutes   *Partner Oral Reading (of yesterday's selection and books of students' choice)*

15 minutes   *Discussion of Yesterday's Selection and/or Student Choices (whole class)*

15 minutes   *Strategy Instruction (whole class)*
Meeting unknown words

15 minutes   *Written Work (partners, small groups, and individual)*
Teacher-directed group (a needs-alike group)
Independent practice
Partner practice

25 minutes   *Projects/Centers*

30 minutes   *Handwriting/Teacher Read-Aloud*

FLEXIBLE GROUPING IN CHELSEA PUBLIC SCHOOLS

At the beginning of the Boston University collaboration with teachers in the Chelsea Public Schools, 70% of children in elementary classrooms were placed in a low-track reading program for instruction. Thirty percent of those children were placed in below grade level texts in the low-track program. Children received substantial extra help through either Chapter 1, bilingual, or special education services. Despite teachers' attempts to meet individual needs by providing supplemental support service and matching materials to instructional needs, 50% of all students in the district performed below grade-appropriate standards on the state assessment. Through the initiative of the superintendent and the principal in one school, teachers agreed to three major changes: (a) Teachers traded in the low-track program for a regular education program, selecting grade-appropriate text for all children and purchasing multiple copies of trade books to integrate with basal reading instruction; (b) Teachers provided special services in-class, rather than within the pull-out model previously used, thus allowing the regular education teacher and the support teacher to co-teach language arts for two hours each day; and (c) To eliminate tracking of students through ability grouping, teachers agreed to implement a flexible-grouping model that integrated whole-class and small-group instruction and involved the use of cooperative learning and peer tutoring strategies.

The change in materials was straightforward. Teachers ordered two types: grade-appropriate basal readers and supplemental children's trade books based on themes in the basal reading program and the content area. To stretch the book-buying dollar, teachers agreed to order all trade books in sets of sixteen, which provided one book for every pair of children (the largest class size was thirty), and one for the teacher.

The shift from pull-out to in-class staffing was more complex. Teachers needed to be teamed with colleagues with whom they could work collaboratively; schedules needed to be staggered so all teachers did not teach language arts at the same time, permitting support teachers to serve more than one classroom; and other curricular programs (e.g., music, physical education, art) needed to be scheduled outside of the two-hour language arts time period. With the help and cooperation of the entire staff, the principal created a schedule to accomplish each of these objectives.

The most complex change was the shift from ability grouping to flexible grouping. Though most of the teachers expressed interest in exploring alternatives to current practices, few had experience with cooperative learning strategies, and most had used a skills-based approach to reading. Therefore, the new plan required staff development to introduce teachers to process-based reading instruction and cooperative learning strategies before the grouping model could be effectively implemented.

This section describes the steps taken to achieve the change from ability grouping to flexible grouping, and provides examples from one third-grade classroom. The flexible-grouping model described is based on current research and theory in effective environments for literacy learning (Allington & McGill-Franzen, 1989; Anderson & Armbruster, 1990; Barr & Dreeben,

1991; Indrisano & Paratore, 1991; Roehler & Duffy, 1991). It integrates the full range of grouping plans, including whole-class instruction, smaller needs-based groups, cooperative groups, peer tutoring, and individual learning. Teachers selected each of these organizational options at various points in the instructional plan.

Implementation was accomplished in two phases, using first a transition model, and later a differentiated-grouping model.

Phase One: Transition Model

The transition phase introduced teachers and students to cooperative learning and peer tutoring strategies, and to some key reading strategies for use in cooperative groups. Reading strategies introduced and practiced with the whole class included making predictions before and during reading; using a story map to recall and discuss the selection; composing a story summary; and using webbing to recall, elaborate on, and organize story details and events in preparation for tasks such as composing character sketches and setting descriptions. During the transitional phase, teachers used trade books considered relatively easy and therefore accessible to every student in the classroom. The instructional framework included the following steps:

➤ 1. The teacher convenes the whole class to introduce new vocabulary and concepts, and to elicit predictions and set purposes about the selection. Often, ideas are recorded on a chalkboard or easel, usually organized graphically through mapping or webbing.

➤ 2. The selection, or part of it, is read aloud to the whole class, while children follow along in their own text. During and following the read-aloud, students consider predictions and questions, and respond and revise as appropriate.

➤ 3. Students read the selection silently.

➤ 4. Students form pairs for partner reading. During partner reading, they alternate pages, reading aloud and helping each other with difficult words or phrases.

➤ 5. Children reconvene as a whole class for further discussion of the text. To guide the discussion, the teacher introduces a reading strategy, such as story mapping or story webbing.

➤ 6. Students make an entry in a response journal about the selection read. Entries are often related to the discussion in Step 5.

➤ 7. Follow-up activities, both small-group and individual, support intertextual connections, leading students to relate the book read to other books and to other curricular areas. In preparation for these activities, children are introduced explicitly to cooperative learning and peer tutoring strategies, as appropriate. Tasks incorporate the reading strategies introduced and practiced earlier during whole-class discussion (Step 5) and also integrate the selection with language arts or content area instruction (e.g., use of story mapping to compare and contrast versions of a fairy tale, development of character sketches for main characters from different selections, or use of details in a historical fiction selection to create a web describing a setting central to a social studies topic). Peer tutoring provides students extra help with a particular skill or strategy.

Phase Two: Differentiated-Grouping Model

Teachers generally chose to spend about four to six weeks using the transition model. During this time, they became familiar with the full range of grouping options, phasing in new practices over time. Initially, teachers relied heavily on peer dyads for cooperative group work. Teachers observed children closely as they worked with partners, and often intervened in group work to introduce and model cooperative learning and group problem-solving strategies as necessary. As they became more confident in students' cooperative learning skills, they slowly increased group size to three or four students.

When the children (and teachers) had acquired some familiarity and facility with the full range of grouping options, some key reading strategies, and cooperative learning strategies, the differentiated-grouping model was implemented. This model incorporates the strategies described in the transition model and adds a step. Students temporarily join needs-based groups, permitting teacher-directed extra help for some children while the others work individually or in cooperative learning pairs or groups. During this model's implementation time, all children read the same, grade-appropriate text. A typical instructional sequence looks like this:

➤ **1.** The teacher convenes the whole class to introduce new vocabulary and concepts, elicit predictions, and set purposes about the selection. Often, ideas are recorded on a chalkboard or easel, usually organized graphically through mapping or webbing. This step frequently incorporates cooperative learning as students form pairs to make predictions or set purposes for reading.

➤ **2.** Following the whole-class lesson, two smaller groups are formed on the basis of individual needs. One group consists of those who had the background knowledge, interest, and reading proficiency to read and respond to the selection independently and/or in student-led groups. In the other group are students who need extra help with either vocabulary or concepts to understand the selection fully. These groups are flexible, formed on the basis of the particular selection to be read. Tasks for groups included these steps:

Individual Learning and Student-Led Groups

a. Students read selection silently.
b. Cooperative response groups discuss selection and develop a written product.
c. Students form cooperative pairs and select a passage of approximately one-hundred words to read to each other.
d. Students self-select thematically related literature for independent reading.

Teacher-Led Groups and Cooperative Pairs

a. The teacher reads the selection in whole or in part.
b. The teacher reaches and reviews vocabulary.
c. Students read the selection silently.
d. Students reread the selection aloud in cooperative pairs.

→ 3. The teacher reconvenes the whole class, or students form heterogeneous cooperative learning groups, to discuss the selection, compare it to those read previously, and/or engage in group writing.

→ 4. Small groups again are formed.

Teacher-Facilitated Needs-Based Group

a. With the teacher, students share and discuss the cooperative learning task completed earlier.
b. Students discuss the self-selected readings and relate them to target selection.

Student-Led Cooperative Pairs and Groups

a. Individually or in pairs, students compose a written response to the selection.
b. Students select "easy" books for practice and application.

→ 5. Follow-up activities vary widely, and include the formation of (a) cooperative learning groups to extend the selection or the topic through other reading and writing tasks, (b) whole or cooperative learning groups to integrate the selection with language arts or content area instruction, (c) tutoring pairs to provide students extra help with a particular skill or strategy, and (d) teacher-led groups to provide introductory or review instruction in a particular skill or strategy.

Discussion and Outcomes

Shifting away from ability grouping toward a flexible grouping model was not easy. Successful implementation required teachers to become familiar with cooperative learning and peer tutoring strategies. Teachers needed patience as children became skilled at interacting with their peers in ways that promoted, rather than distracted from, learning. After a year of implementation teachers widely agreed, however, that the change was beneficial. Anecdotal data gathered from classroom observations and teacher interviews suggest there are four important outcomes: (a) increased expectations for all students, (b) equality of opportunity for all students, (c) easier integration of the language arts, and (d) easier integration of language arts with other curricular areas. Examples of each of these outcomes follow.

Increased Expectations for All Students. As noted previously, at the end of the last school year approximately 70% of the children in this school received instruction in reading in low-track or below grade level text. These practices resulted in different curricular goals and lower expectations for students, impacting both their self-esteem and their achievement. A shift toward a heterogeneous grouping model promoted increased expectations for all students, as teachers accepted the responsibility to explore ways to make the grade-appropriate curriculum accessible to all students, rather than alter it. Instead of changing the text to meet individual needs, teachers scaffolded instruction, using strategies such as previewing, reading aloud, and providing opportunities for rereading and vocabulary review. Peer instruction satisfied the need for varying degrees of help. Ultimately, scaffolding led to "easier" text and greater accessibility for all children.

Evidence of the increased expectations can be seen both in the placement and the performance of students. Every third-grade child in the classroom was placed in grade-appropriate text. While children needed varied amounts of extra help, every child engaged in oral rereading of all or some of the text, every child composed written responses to the text, and every child had an opportunity to read beyond the text. As noted, this supplementary reading comprised sometimes challenging and sometimes less difficult text. Adequacy of performance was judged by word recognition accuracy during oral rereading, contributions to oral discussions, and written responses recorded in reading journals. Work samples demonstrated, as expected in a heterogeneously grouped classroom, there was clearly a range of student performance. However, when adequate support and extra help were provided, every student participated with some level of success.

The following examples of work are illustrative. For this lesson, the common text was Byrd Baylor's *Hawk, I'm Your Brother*. After reading, rereading, and discussing the selection, students were asked to form cooperative pairs and compose the dialogue the character, Rudy Soto, and the hawk may have engaged in at the story's end. The writing sample presented in Figure 3-2 represents the work of two students who would have been placed in the high reading group of a traditionally organized classroom. Their entry is carefully composed and accurate in spelling and punctuation, and uses

Jessica   & David

Hawk: Thank you for letting me go.
Rudy: Will you ever forgive me for
       taking you.
Hawk: I know it was hard for you to
       let me go.
Rudy: I hope you feel better soaring
       freely than being locked in a cage.
Hawk: I think what you did, took
       alot of courage.
Rudy: I hope someday I will be able to
       fly with you and your brothers.
Hawk: Rudy I think you are old
       enough to know you can only
       fly in your dreams.
Rudy: I know I can't but I will
       never give up my dream.
Hawk: I hope you will never give
       up that dream because if you lose
       your dream I'll lose you.

FIGURE 3-2   Writing Sample from High Achievers

story events in a sequential and relatively straightforward way. The writing sample provided in Figure 3-3 represents the work of two students who, in a traditionally grouped classroom, would not have been assigned this grade level selection since they were judged to be below grade level readers. Consistent with the flexible-grouping model, prior to composing this work sample, they had explicit instruction and practice in key vocabulary, and read the selection three times instead of once. Their written dialogue contains an array of spelling, punctuation, and sentence construction errors. It also, however, demonstrates creative thinking, humor, and thoughtful dialogue between the two characters. In reviewing the samples, their teachers noted that on the criterion "critical thinking and creative response," Mike and Tony may, in fact, have surpassed their "higher performing peers." On

Mike

Hawk : thank you for letting free Rudy ~~d would rather see~~ a true ~~bird fly than~~ me
Rudy: Will you ever forgive
Hawk: give me - time to think about it
Hawk: I'm gest joking I do forgive you you.

Rudy: Will I ever see you again
Hawk: I hope so, If I do I'll introduce you to my brothers.
Rudy: I'm ~~really sorry for tung you up and putting you~~ in a cage.
hawk: that's o.k.
Rudy: Go Fly bird bye
hawk: See you later.

FIGURE 3-3 Writing Sample from Low Achievers

the criterion" understands and uses accurate spelling, punctuation, and sentence structure," they continue to need explicit instruction and support. The flexible-grouping model allows teachers to work on the range of needs students have, without restricting them to particular texts or groups.

Equality of Opportunity for All Students. Underlying heterogeneous grouping is an assumption that every child has the right to have access to the standard curriculum of a classroom or a school system. By modifying the way teachers introduced and practiced the text, rather than changing the text itself, teachers made a commitment to have the goals and objectives of the "regular" classroom program accessible to every child.

Teachers became so convinced they were able to scaffold instruction for every child that, seven months into the school year, the only child from the third-grade classroom who remained in a substantially separate, special education program was brought in for language arts instruction, rather than pulled out. When this particular student integrated into the regular education program, teachers observed that, with scaffolded instruction, he, too, was able to accomplish what peers could. In another case, a parent expressed concerns that her child had always had pull-out instruction in the past, and was entitled to it now. The co-teachers outlined exactly how they provided the child more help in the current model, and passionately argued for (and eventually received) approval to keep the child in the regular classroom. Such a commitment promotes and supports equality of opportunity for all students.

"Easier" Integration of the Language Arts. The differences in grouping practices used in reading and the language arts had often led previously to separate instruction in these curricular areas. Different instructional materials, instructional times, and often instructional settings made effective or systematic integration difficult. As the reading instructional setting more closely resembles the language arts instructional setting, integration becomes a natural outgrowth. So, for example, when all students read *Hawk, I'm Your Brother*, this text becomes the context for language arts instruction. Dialogue writing, an upcoming language arts skill, is taught within the context of response to literature. Children are asked to form pairs and compose a dialogue between Hawk and Rudy Soto (see Figure 3-2 and 3-3). In a traditionally grouped reading class, this integration would be more difficult, since different groups of children would read different text, and the multi-ability pairs would not share the same knowledge of the selection used to generate the dialogue.

On a simpler level, the teachers join instruction in cursive writing with the reading curriculum, as children are asked to practice new letter forms using key words from selections they had read. In another lesson, they used Sarah, the main character from Patricia MacLachlan's *Sarah, Plain and Tall*, as the practice word for the letter "S." The outcome of such instruction is the joining of reading and the language arts into a unified whole.

Increased Opportunities for Integrating Reading and the Language Arts with Other Curricular Areas. Just as heterogeneous grouping promotes integration of reading with the language arts, it also promotes integration with other curricular areas. For example, when all students participate in the reading selection of an excerpt from Patricia Lauber's *Journey to the Planets*, the experience becomes the starting point for instruction in a science curriculum unit on planets. Similarly, a reading of Jean Fritz's *The Cabin Faced West* formed the basis of discussion for an important aspect of American history. When children in a class share a reading/language arts curriculum, such joining and integration throughout the classroom day comes naturally.

The grouping model used as the primary instructional framework at the Williams School in Chelsea, Massachusetts, is not intended to represent the only context for literacy learning. On the contrary, teachers continue to explore other learning contexts, using cooperative learning groups for Book Club discussions (Pardo & Raphael, 1991), individual learning for Reading Workshop (Reutzel & Cooter, 1991), and peer tutoring pairs for Reciprocal Teaching (Palincsar & Brown, 1984; Palincsar & David, 1991). The model presented here, however, provides one way to organize instruction at those times when teachers wish to have all students read and respond to a single text beyond the level of independence for some children.

FLEXIBLE GROUPING IN DADE COUNTY

Dade County Public Schools (Miami, Florida) is known for its schoolbased management. Flexible grouping in Dade County has many forms, varying greatly from school to school and even within schools. The general direction has been encouragement to begin each period with whole-class instruction, move to flexible grouping, and conclude with the whole class. District emphasis focuses on ways of meeting the needs of students above and below grade level with such strategies as cooperative learning, repeated readings, the simultaneous use of two levels for low achievers, and the use of early bird instruction as needed—before introducing the class as a whole to a selection (see Chapter 2). The following description of several classrooms in one elementary school illustrates Dade County's diversity.

Flexible Grouping at Frederick Douglass Elementary School

One sample of plan variety in Dade County is Frederick Douglass Elementary, at the time of this writing an inner-city, 1,300-student primary school, with 97% of the students receiving free and reduced-cost breakfast and lunch. Stanford Achievement Test median reading scores are below the 33rd percentile. The school represents two distinct populations, 71% Hispanic and 28% Black Non-Hispanic. Sixty-two percent of Douglass's population receives ESOL services, mainly in self-contained ESOL classrooms. Douglass classrooms have computers and extensive classroom libraries of predictable and other books purchased with Chapter 1 funds.

Douglass has six teachers for forty-eight classrooms. Included in this group are thirty-eight support teachers, a Chapter 1 lead teacher, and three reading resource specialists, paid for through a schoolwide Chapter 1 program and through schoolbased management funds. The need to juggle this staff led the school to be flexible in its overall approach to scheduling, even before the issue of flexible grouping within the classroom arose.

Douglass uses a block schedule, in which two uninterrupted hours each day are given for language arts. According to the needs of the students and the personalities and comfort level of the teachers working together, several grouping plans developed. Douglass's support teachers reduced student-teacher ratios by working in all Grade 1–3 classrooms for one hour in the two-hour reading/language arts block with the exception of the two teachers who did not wish to have that support.

All five grouping options discussed in Chapter 2 (whole-class instruction, teacher-facilitated needs-based groups, cooperative groups, pairs, and individual teaching and learning) are used at Douglass. Following are discussions of flexible grouping as it occurred in classes of teachers who were comfortable with the plan. Different types of classes are included. Teachers at Douglass are now trying to fine-tune their grouping so that in each class different grouping options are used to meet varying curricular goals and individual needs.

Eight Kindergarten Classes.   Eight kindergarten classes deliver initial instruction in whole classes with small-group and individual follow-up. The kindergarten teachers plan together once a week. Each have four structured centers in addition to a home center and a library corner. These centers are all developmentally appropriate with child-sized furniture and plentiful manipulatives. All students visit the four structured centers (math, content area, language arts, and writing) every day. Each classroom is divided into four groups of five to eight students. Each group is responsible for completing an activity in each center. Students move through the centers every 15–20 minutes, working independently or in small groups on listening, speaking, reading, and writing activities related to the overall theme of the current unit.

Sandra Banky's Grade 1 Class.   Sandra Banky's regular first-grade class used flexible grouping for the previous two years. Her grouping patterns are varied. Language arts lessons begin with whole-class instruction. Children then separate into groups of three to four for follow-up activities, projects, or paired readings, or for more concentrated instruction from Ms. Banky. Meanwhile, support teacher Delphinia Walcott pulls flexible groups for skills, rereading, or special projects with above grade level readers. Children are grouped by interest when instructional centers are used. Sometimes, groupings self-select. Ms. Banky's children write cooperatively and independently. Children often discuss their writing ideas and edit each other's writing.

Ross Pivnik's Grade 2 ESOL Class. Students in Ross Pivnik's self-contained second-grade ESOL class receive a much-needed chance to master basic sight vocabulary and achieve levels of fluency primarily through page partner reading. Mr. Pivnik works from the Grade 1 rather than Grade 2 text. Although he uses several other grouping options and activities, it is his page partner reading we will focus on here. After repeated readings by the teacher and the whole class, students pair up to read a story, simply taking turns reading pages to each other and helping each other with decoding or comprehension problems. Mr. Pivnik matches his partners informally and heterogeneously. The pairs, or sometimes triads, work in short frequent sessions.

Luz Torres's Grade 2 ESOL Class. Luz Torres, a Douglass Teacher of the Year, has a Grade 2 self-contained ESOL class. During the first hour of her two-hour language arts block, she instructs the whole class with such activities as building selection background, activating prior knowledge, teaching vocabulary, reading the selection aloud, teaching a literature-based phonics strategy, or implementing a strategy. During the second hour of instruction, Ms. Torres is assisted by Elaine Calderalo, a support teacher. At this time, the teachers have four fixed heterogeneous groups of eight students, with each teacher responsible for two of these groups. Teachers spend a total of 30 minutes with a group; in a two-day period, all four groups are seen. The teachers use needs-based groups to cover areas such as: intensive vocabulary reviews, follow-up on literature-based phonics instruction, story rereading, study skills, and writing activities. Independent groups read the core selection silently, complete vocabulary notebooks, select a story to read, perform self-selected writing, practice buddy reading, or complete projects related to the reading selection.

Rose Llera's Grade 2 Academic Excellence Class. Rose Llera's Grade 2 academic excellence class for high achievers does a lot of work with cooperative learning, buddy reading, and writing process. Students engage in peer conferences during planning, revising, and editing stages. Team practice usually follows lessons on language mechanics and language expression activities related to the students' writings. Ms. Llera's support teacher, Elvira Alonzo, works with writing instruction, an area she is more comfortable with than reading. Ms. Alonzo manages a collaborative writing center in the class. For one hour during the language arts block, she helps students revise and edit favorite pieces of writing taken from any area of the curriculum.

Terri Murray's Grade 3 Academic Excellence Class.   Terri Murray's third-grade academic excellence class works extensively with cooperative learning. Ms. Murray defines the desired collaborative and academic skills, sets up group size (usually two students), and forms groups with students heterogeneously mixed by ability, gender, and interest. She arranges the room so students in a group face each other, with each group slightly apart from other groups. Each student's specific role (e.g., reader, recorder) is clearly defined on an index card.

Examples of expected behaviors are modeled before groups set up. For each task students receive necessary background material and examples. Group members resolve their own problems. Processing is ongoing, with Ms. Murray "clipboard cruising" as she listens for interaction, oral summarization, and explanations, gives words of encouragement, and evaluates performance. The groups process their activities with questions such as "How well did we work together?" "Did everyone contribute?" "What worked well?" and "What did not work?" Students conclude cooperative activities by listing things done well and things that could have been done better.

Christina Nodarse's Grade 3 At-Risk Class.   Christina Nodarse uses predictable book lessons with ten third graders who started the year as nonreaders while her support teacher, Viola Torrent, instructs the remainder of the class with the grade level text. Some of Ms. Nodarse's ESOL students are in each group. Except for the end of each period when Ms. Nodarse's children show off their reading for the rest of the class, this room is essentially conducted as two classes. Ms. Nodarse's group does not read the grade level book at all. After shared reading with the predictable books, she works with half of her small group while the others work at learning centers; her students later rotate. Ms. Torrent uses some cooperative learning and some skill-group instruction with her students; she pulls skill groups while other students work with paired reading or with cooperative writing assignments.

Beth Kibler's Intermediate LD Class.   Beth Kibler, a second-year teacher, has been selected as the district LD Rookie Teacher of the Year and is a district model for other LD teachers. Despite extremely tight quarters, a hectic schedule, and more than thirty students, she manages to have junior entomologists, charts on the growth of chicken eggs, trade books galore, computers always on the go, and books constantly in production. She uses a reading/writing workshop approach (Calkins, 1986), spending about two weeks on a theme. Ms. Kibler starts with read-alouds and shared reading, and moves into groupings of two to three. Her groups are sometimes heterogeneously mixed by ability, but she also lets higher achievers work together at times. Personalities form a key factor in the class's grouping decisions. Ms. Kibler allows students to make many of the lesson-plan decisions and finds a good deal of student buy-in as a result.

Reading Reentry: A Reading Intervention Program. At the time of this writing, Douglass also participates in Dade County's Reading Reentry, an intervention program that builds on some of the effective strategies included in Clay's (1987) *Reading Recovery*. Douglass has eight Reading Reentry tutors who work one-on-one with a small number of the weakest first-grade readers. This includes two pairs of first-grade teachers who share a class; each teacher gives Reading Reentry lessons half the day. These teachers are also able to incorporate Reading Reentry principles when teaching all their children. The remaining four tutors are the three resource teachers and the Chapter 1 lead teacher, all of whom provide Reading Reentry lessons part of the day.

As the examples show, Douglass has made a good start toward flexible grouping.

SUMMARY OF THE THREE PLANS

In these three plans, teachers made a decision to provide core instruction from a grade-appropriate basal or trade book selection, with regular supplemental use of self-selected reading.

There are many commonalities among the three experiences. Each uses a variety of grouping structures to meet curricular goals and individual needs. Each shares common reading strategies: teacher read-alouds, repeated readings, and written response. The Chelsea and Dade models shift from pull-out to in-class staffing. In all three models, teachers are encouraged to experiment and take risks. Finally, all three experienced similar outcomes: increased expectations for all students, equality of opportunity for all students, easier integration of the language arts, and increased opportunities for integrating reading and the language arts with other curricular areas.

CONCLUDING REMARKS

Organizing students for instruction in reading and language arts consumes a major part of every elementary teacher's planning. In this chapter we have provided three plans which demonstrate how grouping options may be combined when students share a single, grade-appropriate text. Chapter 4 describes models in which children read multiple rather than single texts.

REFERENCES

Allington, R. L., & McGill-Franzen, A. (1989). Different programs, indifferent instruction. In D. K. Lipsky & A. Gartner (Eds.), *Beyond separate education: Quality education for all* (pp. 75–98). Baltimore: Paul H. Brookes.

Anderson, R. C., & Armbruster, B. B. (1990). Some maxims for learning and instruction. *Teachers College Record, 16*, 85–96.

Barr, R., & Dreeben, R. (1991). Grouping students for reading instruction. In R. Barr, M. L. Kamil, P. Mosenthal, & P. D. Pearson (Eds.), *Handbook of reading research* (Vol. II). New York: Longman.

Calkins, L. M. (1986). *The art of teaching writing*. Portsmouth, NH: Heinemann.

Clay, M. M. (1987). *The early detection of reading difficulties*. Portsmouth, NH: Heinemann.

Cunningham, P. M. (1991a). *Phonics they use: Words for reading and writing*. New York: HarperCollins.

Cunningham, P. M. (1991b). Research directions: Multimethod, multilevel literacy instruction in first grade. *Language Arts, 68*, 578–584.

Cunningham, P. M., & Hall, D. P. (1991). Non-ability-grouped, multilevel instruction: A year in a first-grade classroom. *The Reading Teacher, 44*, 566–571.

Indrisano, R., & Paratore, J. R. (1991). Classroom contexts for literacy learning. In J. Flood, J. M. Jensen, D. Lapp, & J. R. Squire (Eds.), *Handbook of research on teaching the English language arts* (pp. 477–488). New York: Macmillan.

Palincsar, A. S., & Brown, A. L. (1984). Reciprocal teaching of comprehension-fostering and comprehension-monitoring activities. *Cognition and Instruction, 1*, 117–175.

Palincsar, A. S., & David, Y. M. (1991). Promoting literacy through classroom dialogue. In E. H. Hiebert (Ed.), *Literacy for a diverse society: Perspectives, practices, and policies* (pp. 122–140). New York: Teachers College Press.

Pardo, L. S., & Raphael, T. E. (1991). Classroom organization for instruction in content areas. *The Reading Teacher, 44*, 556–565.

Reutzel, D. R., & Cooter, R. B. (1991). Organizing for effective instruction: The reading workshop. *The Reading Teacher, 44*, 548–554.

Roehler, L. R., & Duffy, G. G. (1991). Teachers' instructional actions. In R. Barr, M. L. Kamil, P. Mosenthal, & P. D. Pearson (Eds.), *Handbook of reading research* (Vol. II). New York: Longman.

Strickland, D. S. (1992). Organizing a literature-based reading program. In B. E. Cullinan (Ed.), *Invitation to read: More children's literature in the reading program.* Newark, DE: International Reading Association.

Wiggins, R. A. (1994). Large group lesson/small group follow-up: Flexible grouping in a basal reading program. *The Reading Teacher, 47,* 450–460.

CHILDREN'S BOOKS

Baylor, B. (1976). *Hawk, I'm your brother.* New York: Charles Scribner's Sons.

Fritz, J. (1958). *The cabin faced west.* New York: Crown.

Lauber, P. (1982). *Journey to the planets.* New York: Scholastic.

MacLachlan, P. (1985). *Sarah, plain and tall.* New York: HarperCollins.

Mattingly, C. (1986). *Duck Boy.* New York: Atheneum.

▶ 4

Literature Circles for the Teaching of Literature-Based Reading

WENDY C. KASTEN

In one corner of a 2/3 multiage classroom, five children are on the floor in the classroom reading corner, set off by two freestanding bookcases and an area rug. These second and third graders are reading Patricia MacLachlan's novel, *Sarah, Plain and Tall*. They share the story aloud with each other, then write personal responses in nearby journal notebooks. Later they will share what they wrote.

These are literature circles, one type of flexible grouping. They consist of a group of mixed-ability children who select the same book (a good novel or picture book), engage in the intimate act of reading the story aloud to each other, write their reactions and feelings in a response journal, and share their ideas in a discussion. The children meet this way up to several weeks, about 30 minutes at a time, until their book is completely read. Some children will read aloud often. Others, who are more reticent to read aloud, will be good listeners. Once they reach the end of their book, the students begin to negotiate a way to share something the story has meant to them with the rest of the class.

WHY LITERATURE CIRCLES INSTEAD OF BASAL READING GROUPS?

In today's elementary classrooms, children have a wide variety of reading abilities and interests whether the class is a single grade, such as a second grade, or whether the class represents multiage groupings of two or more traditional age groups intermingled (such as a grade 2/3, 4/5, or even a K/1/2/3). However children have been grouped, there are diverse reading abilities, often spanning from emergent readers to fluent accomplished readers, in a single class. This is both typical and normal from a child-development perspective. Literature circles help to accommodate these disparities.

Another reason for using literature circles is the realization by today's teachers that it is no longer sufficient only to teach children *how* to read if we don't also teach them *what* to read, with a strong desire to do so. Consequently, many classrooms have libraries over and above the basal reader selections. In spite of monumental improvements to the basal's quality of literature, there are still limited choices and selections in any basal, especially when compared to the wider variety available in the school library. To accommodate children's tastes, infuse the curriculum with more, high-quality selections, and coordinate reading material with classroom content themes, many teachers provide part or all of their reading instruction with children's trade books. With the wealth of quality literature available, this practice can more readily accommodate classroom needs for varying interests and topics. Some teachers continue to use a basal with quality selections of literature, while others teach entirely with children's trade books and novels.

This chapter will outline ways to teach reading with quality literature when children have diverse reading needs and not everyone in the class reads the same selection. A class of twenty-eight children might have six or seven novels or stories being read at one time—and the children are *not* always grouped by reading ability, a practice that has been questioned particularly for its affective results on readers (see Chapter 1). The main perspective of this chapter focuses on literature circles for children who already have attained some independence in reading. In other words, for the most part, the readers can read fluently. A variation for emergent readers will be discussed later in this chapter.

Also, I will describe literature circles when trade books are used. Noting that everything described here can be adapted for use with a quality short story found in a basal reader, the chapter will discuss techniques to use picture books and chapter books as reading material.

To minimize misunderstandings, I reiterate that literature circles are not traditional reading groups. Literature circles do not use the outdated practice of round-robin reading. Literature circles differ profoundly from round-robin reading practices. Aside from the issue of teacher presence, discussed later under "The Teacher's Role," a second difference is that children read aloud by choice. Sometimes better readers may do all the reading. At other times, the group may decide how and when to take turns. Readers who come to something they do not know how to pronounce are helped by the group, rather than corrected by them.

 One last caveat: Although literature circles may form a great deal of the reading program's core, they do not replace other methods of direct instruction needed for developing diverse reading skills. For example, since the focus of literature circles is on deeper comprehension, this strategy might replace other comprehension strategies at least some of the time, such as questioning at the end of a selection. However, some readers who participate in literature circles as listeners may not yet be fluent readers and may need guided reading (Renwick, 1985) and other direct instruction to increase their understanding of how our language works. Even among fluent readers, there will be a need for instruction in the reading of expository text, with strategies aimed at retrieving information, such as recognizing main ideas. No comprehensive reading program should be limited only to the reading of the narrative.

RETHINKING "LEVELS"

As teachers, we once thought it important that children always read on their own reading "level," a product of a score from tests administered to them. Although we were right to want to avoid frustrating struggling readers, there were other factors we hadn't taken into account.

In rethinking reading levels, one consideration is children's widespread watching of television and movies (for better or for worse). Children watch the same movies and television programs adults watch (even when we wish they wouldn't). There are no prime-time television programs written down to the levels of children, as reading materials sometimes are. Consequently, children are exposed to the same vocabulary and sentence structure in these oral texts as are their teachers and parents. Yet children repeatedly give these programs and movies their full attention for extended periods of time and comprehend the stories communicated.

Often, especially with struggling readers, intellectual capacity far exceeds reading ability. Readers can hear and use language with a great deal more sophistication than they can maneuver in their personal reading. Poor reading ability and late-blooming reading ability do not necessarily correspond to poorer intellectual abilities. Restricting poor readers only to material they can read independently is delimiting. Under those circumstances, poor readers would naturally find more mental stimulation from television than from books, and that is not the lesson we wish them to learn.

For decades, we have been thinking of readers in terms of the "levels" we created. For the purposes of literature circles, we must set aside that thinking to some extent, and think about good books, mixed groups of children, and sharing the richness of wonderful literature.

DEFINING LITERATURE CIRCLES

Literature circles are groups of three to five children reading a quality book or story together. The members of the literature circle or group are of varied abilities in reading, but may be interested in the same book. Different classrooms call literature circles by different names, such as literature discussion groups, book groups, book clubs, and literary circles. As stated earlier, these groups should typically be heterogeneous, although there may be times when a teacher wishes to group very proficient readers for a challenging selection, or group some struggling readers to give specific instruction for a period of time.

Although definitions of literature circle tasks vary, the definition used here begins with the books being read aloud by volunteering group members in a nook, at a table, or in a corner of the classroom. During every available literature circle time, three activities take place: reading, literature response in journals, and discussion within the group.

For example, in a 50-minute teaching block, there may be six groups meeting separately. Each group reads their books quietly aloud for perhaps 30 minutes, writes thoughts in relationship to the story for perhaps six minutes, and shares journal entries and discusses story events and their feelings about the stories for the rest of the available time.

PROMOTING CRITICAL THINKING WITH BOOKS

Teachers have always been concerned about children understanding what they read. Within the context of literature circles, the teacher aims to promote deeper engagement with texts, to recognize multiple ways of knowing that go far beyond traditional questioning, and to recognize different kinds of intelligences (Gardner, 1983). Multiple intelligences are tapped especially during the last phase of literature circles, after the students have completed the entire book or story. Students are instructed to come up with, as a group, some manner of sharing with their classmates or other classes what the book or story meant to them. This culminates as a presentation that may involve visual arts, media, music, dramatics, storytelling, or pantomime.

Students are further instructed never to give away the story in their presentations, so as perhaps to entice other readers to visit their selection. All group members must be participants in some way, shape, or form. Students of diverse abilities, talents, interests, and ages lend different kinds of support, expertise, and participation to their groups.

All veteran teachers have experienced children with difficulties in reading but who have highly developed or potential talents in, for example, the visual arts. That is not to say artistically talented children should bear all the burden of the artistic nature of the presentations, only that the sum total of activities surrounding the literature circle experience enable children with a wide variety of abilities to feel successful and make worthwhile contributions. Certainly, teachers who are skilled facilitators will want children at times to do what they do best, and at other times to do something new and challenging. Less capable readers who are budding artists may use their artistic talents, still read aloud if they choose to, and still write in their journals to the best of their ability. All students in each group need to participate in all phases of literature circles.

Literature circle experiences can become substantial, enriching parts of classroom life that go far beyond typical reading objectives. Borders and Naylor (1993, p. xii) believe story, and the examination of story, are ways "to make meaning of human existence" and that literature experiences "reverberate in our lives and can act as a stimulus for the development of intellect and character" as well as critical thinking. Peterson and Eeds (1990, pp. 5–6) echo these thoughts when they say that "life in literature-based classrooms is in a constant state of becoming," and that teaching and learning with literature is important because "story is an exploration and illumination of life." Both sets of authors recognize and appreciate the richness of teaching with real books in elementary schools.

Literature circles also make use of cooperative and collaborative learning. Much of what we have come to understand about learning shows us the power of working together (Vygotsky, 1978; Wells & Chang-Wells, 1992), causing us to rethink and in many cases discard past practices that focused on "do your own work" directives (Kasten & Clarke, 1986), especially as the main strategy on the classroom menu. Literature circles enable students to read together: More proficient readers become models for less proficient readers. Literature circles promote peer discussion; children learn from each other's ideas and grow from the exposure. Literature circles promote negotiation of ideas, a skill needed in life and in the workplace. Literature circles promote ways of expressing comprehension, other than, and in addition to, verbal ones. Children whose learning styles and talents lie less within the verbal and communication realms, but who have other talents, can express their comprehension and participation in valid ways and reap the rewards of that participation.

SETTING UP LITERATURE CIRCLES

Some teachers report it may be useful to begin literature circles with one or two heterogeneous groups of individuals with fairly good cooperative skills. These groups set the tone, act as role models, and establish modes of operation prior to including all class members. One teacher in a K/1/2/3 multiage class made literature circles a privilege for more accomplished readers that developing readers could look forward to joining as they became ready.

Here is one way in which literature circles might be implemented.

➤ **1.** Choose five to seven appropriate novels for the ages and interests of a class that represent excellent choices of children's literature. Make a short book talk or presentation about each book, mentioning some of the content or major themes. Perhaps read the brief on the back cover to the class, or draw from your own experience if you have read the selection. This may be done at one time, during the course of the day, or over several days. Meanwhile, also review the class schedule to allot several time slots in the weekly plans for literature circle time.

➤ **2.** Allow children a way of signing up for their first choice, second choice, and perhaps third choice to provide teacher flexibility in creating groups that will work well together. Make it clear that when fewer than three people sign up for a book, the title will not be available at this time, but may be in the future. Use children's choices to balance the groups somewhat in size, varied abilities, and good group dynamics. Generally teachers know who, within their own class, will work well together. Use this knowledge to create groups that have a fair chance of success, which may mean using pupils' second or third choices in some cases.

➤ **3.** Review with students the procedures for running the circles. In most cases, insist that some reading, some journal writing, and some discussion take place each time. For example, if 40 minutes are allotted for literature group time, you may set 20 minutes aside for reading, or designate the amount of reading as one or two chapters. The length of chapters varies greatly among books. Consequently, a time limit might be more useful. Groups may appoint a timekeeper to keep track of reading time.

➤ **4.** Set aside about 6 or 7 minutes for writing in journals. Insist that children write in their journals immediately upon completion of that day's reading and before any discussion takes place. Children are instructed to write *whatever they are thinking about in relationship to the book* in a journal designated for this purpose. Make it clear there are no right answers, but that they will be asked to consider sharing their writing with their groups. After a designated period of writing time, have students begin discussion by reading or talking about what they wrote.

Be sure to set ground rules for sharing. No class member should react negatively to another student's response. It may be necessary to model supportive language as well as appropriate and inappropriate responses when introducing literature circles for the first time. For example, books may cause children to think of something personal in their own life and write about that. From a critical literacy perspective, this is a highly desirable student response. Class members may need to be taught to give supportive comments and to be accepting of and sensitive to a wide range of responses and ideas.

Journals may be the most difficult part of these literature circles. Many children are already accustomed to the canned responses sought by teachers and will respond cautiously and safely with what they like about the book, or with a summary of the book. Teachers who write in their own journals often find this modeling to be a powerful means of moving children away from canned responses. To move away from book report-style writing, some teachers set the guideline that students *cannot* begin their response "I like this book because . . ." Interesting journal responses pave the way for more intriguing discussions.

➤ **5.** Have groups proceed with reading, writing, and discussion cycles whenever literature circle time is allotted. Longer books, such as novels, will take several weeks to complete. Times available for literature circles will vary with each teacher's unique schedule. Often, group time may need to be interrupted by lunch, recess, or special classes. This does not appear to pose a problem for most children. Some teachers allow literature circle time daily. Others begin with two or three times per week to feel their way slowly, perhaps holding literature circles as an initial experiment for a few weeks or as a rest from a basal reading program.

➤ **6.** Have plans for groups that complete books more quickly than others. These groups may be allotted additional planning time for their group presentation, or may not meet as a group for a few days while other groups catch up, reading independently for a period instead, or engaging in other appropriate classroom activities. Some teachers like to set aside one day of celebration where all groups make presentations. Other teachers set two days or more for presentations, allowing faster-paced groups to present sooner. Generally, it would be useful to allow all groups to come to closure before beginning a new literature circle round. The new cycle may begin immediately or after taking a break from the routine. Some titles may be repeated in a subsequent grouping, whereas some new titles should also be available.

━━▶ **7.** Allow time for groups to plan and negotiate class presentations; set guidelines for length. Presentations reflect what the story meant to group members. If possible, videotape them. This will increase the excitement as well as provide an archive for the class (and for future classes) to watch. Acting out scenes from the book is the most popular medium. Others include making videos, dioramas, musical ballads, puppets, shadow plays, radio plays, and narrated murals.

Watching these groups work toward their presentation can be illuminating for teachers. Student discussions and even arguments give clues as to student level of comprehension and, at times, misconceptions. One sixth-grade group decided to make a diorama of "Terabithia" from Katherine Paterson's *Bridge to Terabithia*. All elements of their diorama that were real, students elected to color with paint or crayon. All elements in the scene judged to be from the characters' imaginations, they decided to paint white.

Another group of fifth-grade special education students designed a set of the "Arsenio Hall Show" to interview the characters from Judy Blume's *Tales of a Fourth Grade Nothing*. The student assigned to be Fudgie chose to behave badly during the performance because, he asserted, that is how he believed the character would have behaved under those circumstances (another comprehension clue for teachers). The student assigned by his group to be Arsenio had appeared less involved during the reading of the book. Yet his questions to the characters during the presentation demonstrated a deep, detailed, and very personal understanding of the family in the story.

In one third-grade group, members elected to draw comiclike frames of major events in the story of MacLachlan's *Sarah, Plain and Tall*. Students added speech balloons to insert character comments and dialogue. One student drew a scene from the story which was implied rather than literal, signaling a very sophisticated level of comprehension. Another student included two characters in the same frame and scene who had never met each other in the actual book; the response signaled to the teacher that this pupil had some misconceptions.

A great deal of comprehending continues to take place during the discussions and planning of the responses to the books. It is very important, with classroom time constraints, that this aspect of literature circles not be forfeited. Planning and discussion causes children to have to think in more depth about character traits, settings, and details such as clothing styles, speech styles, and personalities of characters. Often, skimming of chapters and rereading of sections prove necessary during the planning. These are all comprehension-related activities.

CHOOSING LITERATURE FOR THE PRIMARY GRADES

Whether using stories from picture books or simple chapter books (books with chapters), the selections should be not only high-quality literature, but selections worthy of time, discussion, and the extended time needed to complete the groups' work. Some stories may be too short for literature discussion (such as ones found in curriculum kits used for emergent readers). Other stories may be merely sweet and appealing because of their marvelous fluid use of language, such as Bill Martin's *Brown Bear, Brown Bear, What Do You See?* but contain little substance for discussion.

Some picture books have themes that are provocative or relevant to children's lives. These stories are substantial for holding discussions and reacting in literature response journals. Lucille Clifton's *Everett Anderson's Nine Month Long, A Promise is a Promise* by Robert Munsch and Michael Kusugak, *Charlie Anderson* by Barbara Abercrombie, *Koala Lou* by Mem Fox, *Tar Beach* by Faith Ringgold, *Amazing Grace* by Mary Hoffman, and *Chicken Sunday* by Patricia Polacco, all contain situations children can relate to within their lives and in their families. Other selections, such as *The Wall* by Eve Bunting, *Follow the Drinking Gourd* by Jeanette Winter, and *Sweet Clara and the Freedom Quilt* by Deborah Harris, might be chosen to relate to content area study (in this case American history).

Multiple copies of the books are desirable but not necessary. One or two copies can be shared, since all reading is done aloud, and practice at listening is an important skill to develop. Many teachers have started literature circles with only a handful of single copies of outstanding titles from the library or their personal collections.

Teachers less familiar with current children's literature can seek out a helpful library media specialist to recommend appropriate titles. Book reviews in library and teacher magazines are also sources of good titles, as are suggestions from other teachers.

Selections brought forward by children for possible inclusion should be reviewed carefully by the teacher and offered only if worthy. Some selections are best read alone, or, while wonderful, are not suitable for literature circle purposes.

CHOOSING LITERATURE FOR INTERMEDIATE GRADES

With the wealth of quality juvenile literature available today, teachers have many choices and resources to help them steer young readers to powerful, engaging, and intriguing texts. Again, teachers less familiar with current titles might seek the help of an interested library media specialist. Professional publications such as *Language Arts*, *The Reading Teacher*, and *Hornbook* all contain book reviews. The American Library Association's *Booklinks* can help teachers find common threads in varied titles. Both the International Reading Association and the National Council of Teachers of English have special interest groups in children's literature that teachers can join to receive their helpful publications.

The use of chapter books may begin as early as second or third grade. Shorter novels like MacLachlan's *Sarah, Plain and Tall*, Roald Dahl's *James and the Giant Peach*, Beverly Cleary's *Ramona the Brave*, or John Reynolds Gardiner's *Stone Fox* might be useful starting points. Many excellent inexpensive selections are offered by children's book clubs such as Scholastic, Arrow, and Troll.

Many fourth and fifth graders are capable of more substantial novels, like Paterson's *Bridge to Terabithia*, Elizabeth Speare's *Sign of the Beaver* and *The Witch of Blackbird Pond*, Blume's *Tales of a Fourth Grade Nothing*, Gary Paulsen's *Hatchet*, Carolyn Reeder's *Shades of Gray*, Meindert DeJong's *The House of Sixty Fathers*, Joyce Hansen's *Which Way Freedom?*, Lois Lowry's *Number the Stars*, James Lincoln Collier and Christopher Collier's *My Brother Sam Is Dead*, just to name a few. In selecting material, teachers will want to consider novels that can generate interesting questions and dialogue by students, ones in which they can relate to main characters' dilemmas, and sometimes ones that relate to content area study, such as social studies or science. Teachers will also want to consider age-appropriate material. Many fourth, fifth, and sixth graders begin reading young adult novels. Some themes in young adult literature are more appropriate to adolescents, containing more sophisticated issues. Resources like *Long Ago and Far Away* (Hurst, 1991) list selections for fluent readers and address their level of sophistication to aid teachers as they make choices for the classroom.

Although it is ideal for teachers to preview all selections, this may not be possible initially. Relying on the recommendations of other teachers may fill the gap until time is available to read the books. Rediscovering the world of juvenile literature can be delightful and satisfying. Many popular titles are of wonderful quality. Some selections interesting to children such as series books (Nancy Drew, Baby-Sitters Club, Hardy Boys) are formula-written and lack literary merit. Although these selections are certainly permissible for silent reading times, they lack substantial characterization and depth for instructional purposes.

THE TEACHER'S ROLE

During literature circles, the teacher's role is varied. No longer does the teacher sit and wait for children to complete sections, listen constantly to the children's oral reading, or correct children's miscues. Normally, more than one literature circle functions at the same time.

Making these groups gradually learn to be as independent as possible allows the teacher time to act as troubleshooter, facilitator, and participant, as needed. Some groups may need teacher intervention to help them discuss appropriate cooperative strategies if they are unaccustomed to working together. One teacher in a special education self-contained classroom reported that group progress came slowly and was frustrating at times. Children in his classroom had been accustomed to working primarily on their own, in carrels with little interactive group work.

As in other areas of learning, progress for some individuals may be slow. It is important not to abandon group work because of limited cooperative abilities on the part of some or even many students. That would be about as sensible as suspending the teaching of mathematics because of learner difficulties. Remembering that cooperation is as much a needed skill to be learned in school as anything else, and a skill essential to successful employment later in life, teachers now treat the process of the literature circles with equal importance to the language and comprehension skills being learned.

Since groups in literature circles read mostly on their own, some teachers experience difficulty with individual students in a group who want to prompt words for volunteering readers before those readers have had time to think about an unfamiliar word. Establishing group guidelines can be helpful here. One teacher asks her students to count to ten slowly before prompting, to allow the reader some thinking time. Another teacher posts a lists of strategies that must be completed, in order, before telling another student an unfamiliar word. These might include asking the reader to go back to the beginning of the sentence and make a good guess from context, looking at the initial sound of the unfamiliar word, and attempting to sound the word out, all before prompting is allowed.

When a new literature group is beginning, it may be supportive for the teacher to participate by reading the first chapter to group members. Helping students become familiar with the style of the writing or the use of dialect in a story can get them off to a stronger start.

When all groups are functioning smoothly, it is useful for the teacher to eavesdrop on different groups. Their oral reading, their questions, and their discussions all provide kidwatching moments that illuminate student strengths and weaknesses. For example, while listening in, a teacher may discover that the children appear unfamiliar with a concept brought up in the story; it may be useful to briefly interrupt and explain some urgent missing background information.

Teachers often ask what to do with a child who selects a group with a book that is way too difficult for him or her, or a child who never chooses to read aloud, but only listens. Remember, listening is a powerful lesson. We all understand the contribution of reading aloud to children and its importance throughout a child's life. Listening is also a skill, one that is more often expected than deliberately taught. Less proficient readers may gain a great deal from being listeners. Their participation should be evident in their journal responses and discussions. Often, less experienced readers surprise the group and the teacher during discussion time with their insights.

Thus, the teacher's role during literature circles is that of a rover and facilitator, placing efforts where most needed at any moment.

MORE ABOUT LITERATURE RESPONSE JOURNALS

 Many children are already accustomed to structured materials and limited required responses. Consequently, many teachers find it difficult to move children to take risks in their journals and fully express their thoughts and ideas.

One teacher of a 2/3 multiage class found she needed to explicitly teach lessons about literature responses. For example, one lesson focused on the question, "What does this book make me think about?" Using a picture book read to the class, they discussed, practiced, and shared responses to that question. On another day, they repeated the lesson with, "What in this story reminds me of something else I read?" (or in some cases, what they saw in a movie or television program).

After these lessons, the teacher reported that students within their own group were able to make better responses in their journals. The questions they discussed remained on a reference chart hanging in the classroom for reference if the students needed help deciding what they might write in their journal.

Borders and Naylor (1993, pp. 5–6) experimented with some useful open-ended prompts to help students think about what to write in their literature response journals. These prompts include "Talk about what the story reminds you of in your own life." These prompts often spurred readers to write extensively and relate personal stories that delved deeply into aspects of the book.

Another activity, commonly used in New Zealand and Australian class-rooms, can be used as part of literature responses. *Written conversations* are dialogues on paper about a topic. Children are paired or in triads. One child writes on a paper to a partner sitting nearby. The partner's job is to read what the first child wrote, and respond immediately in writing. During written conversations, talking is not permitted. When using threes in this strategy, each child might write on her or his own paper a question, comment, or idea. Students might then pass their paper clockwise, with each recipient reading the prior student's comment and adding a response. The papers are rotated again so that a third student reads what both predecessors wrote and also adds a response.

Written conversations can continue for 30 minutes in some cases. Students enjoy this strategy, which feels like "passing notes," as children have done on their own forever. An added benefit is the strengthening of the reading/writing connection, as children obviously must read and comprehend their classmate's work to respond.

VARIATIONS FOR EMERGENT READERS

Recently, I attended a conference presentation where kindergarten teachers had developed a way of conducting literature circles with children who were not yet readers. Over the course of a week or ten days, books were sent home with directions for someone to read the book with the child at least twice over the course of several days. Later, back in school, children who read the same book were assembled for discussion and asked to offer their opinions and insights, and sometimes dramatize the story. After a while, teachers reported that parent/home cooperation was very high as was community response to their program.

Using the ideas of these teachers, children whose reading abilities are substantially below that of their class can perhaps have the reading material read to them by an older student or a parent volunteer. This would enable them to participate fully in the discussion of the book or story. It might even be helpful to read the selection several times with emergent readers prior to the literature circle time for sharing and discussion.

Participating in literature circles can help early readers feel like they have joined the "literacy club" (Smith, 1988). Other kinds of more direct instruction, however, will also need to take place, such as shared reading (Holdaway, 1979) in larger groups with a Big Book or a predictable book, and guided reading (Renwick, 1985). Guided reading is done with very simple but predictable books in small groups or individually. It helps children to become more independent at the task of getting meaning from print.

Within literature circles, at-risk readers can still elect to participate in a group, despite their poor skills. These students may not be able to read aloud during reading times, but then again, literature circles respect choice and allow children to choose whether or not they help with oral reading. Poorer readers will benefit greatly from having a copy of the book in front of them so that they can follow along, even if multiple copies are limited.

At-risk readers can be listeners, keep journals along with their class-mates, and participate in all discussions. Since their intellectual capacity often exceeds their reading ability, this may prove to be a very encouraging situation. Often, the insights offered by the less fluent readers are interest-ing, diverse, and even profound. Their life experiences, their ideas, and their voices can find an appropriate audience in a literature circle discussion. Less able readers participate in literature circles at their intellectual level instead of their reading level and have a chance to feel like a valued mem-ber of the group. Often, their participation can be very surprising and infor-mative for their teacher.

PATIENCE WITH CHANGE

As with all new things, change may be slow. Teachers may need to proceed gradually with a strategy that differs from their more practiced way of teach-ing reading. Also, children unaccustomed to group work and cooperation may find it difficult at first. In the beginning, teachers may need to praise and encourage even the smallest gains. Occasionally, teachers find an indi-vidual who resists being part of any group, claiming to prefer to work alone. It may be prudent to honor such a request if a reasonable amount of persua-sion proves unsuccessful. Typically, children of this sort will elect to join a group at a later time, seeing the appeal of the groups at work in the classroom.

It is important to note that social skills, as vital as academic ones, are a key to success in literature circles or any other kind of group work. These skills may have to be discussed and taught at length for some classes, just as any difficult content might need repeated lessons and reinforcement. Often, when teachers assume children can work together and they do not, the out-come is discouraging. However, abandoning group work because of poor social skills will not help these vital skills develop. Since group work is very appealing to most students, some teachers find success treating group mem-bership as a privilege that can be suspended temporarily if group guide-lines are not followed.

Change can be slow, and not all new strategies are immediately success-ful. Patience is important. It may also be useful to analyze and praise as-pects of the literature circles that were very successful and brainstorm solu-tions to problems that may arise along the way, either with the children themselves, with colleagues, or both.

CONCLUDING REMARKS

Literature circles can provide an exciting and deeply engaging manner for teaching reading and literature using multiple selections. The use of high-quality children's literature exposes students to texts they can interact with and relate to. The manner in which circles are conducted can be extremely flexible—to fit nearly any type of class with varied ages, interests, and abilities.

The primary goal of literature circles is to help kids fall in love with books. Students will not likely forget the story they painted, sang, or acted out for their classmates. This and other rich literature experiences can help hook children as lifelong readers.

REFERENCES

Borders, S. G., & Naylor, A. P. (1993). *Children talking about books.* Phoenix, AZ: Oryx Press.

Gardner, H. (1983). *Frames of mind: The theory of multiple intelligences.* New York: HarperCollins.

Holdaway, D. (1979). *The foundations of literacy.* Portsmouth, NH: Heinemann.

Hurst, C. O. (1991). *Long ago and far away.* Allen, TX: Developmental Learning Materials.

Kasten, W. C., & Clarke, B. K. (1986). *A study of 3rd and 5th grade students' oral language during the writing process in elementary classrooms.* Sarasota: University of South Florida. (ERIC Document Reproduction Service No. ED 277025.)

Peterson, R., & Eeds, M. (1990). *Grand conversations.* New York: Scholastic.

Renwick, W. L. (1985). *Reading in junior classes.* Wellington, NZ: Department of Education.

Smith, F. (1988). *Joining the literacy club.* Portsmouth, NH: Heinemann.

Vygotsky, L. (1978). *Mind in society.* Cambridge, MA: Harvard University Press.

Wells, G., & Chang-Wells, G. L. (1992). *Constructing knowledge together.* Portsmouth, NH: Heinemann.

CHILDREN'S BOOKS

Abercrombie, B. (1990). *Charlie Anderson.* New York: Margaret K. McElderry Books.

Blume, J. (1972). *Tales of a fourth grade nothing.* New York: Dell.

Bunting, E. (1990). *The wall.* New York: Clarion Books.

Cleary B. (1975). *Ramona the brave.* New York: Scholastic.

Clifton, L. (1978). *Everett Anderson's nine month long.* New York: Henry Holt.

Collier, J. L., & Collier, C. C. (1974). *My brother Sam is dead.* New York: Scholastic.

Dahl, R. (1961). *James and the giant peach.* New York: Knopf.

DeJong, M. (1956). *The house of sixty fathers.* New York: Harper & Row.

Fox, M. (1988). *Koala Lou.* New York: Harper & Row.

Gardiner, J. R. (1980). *Stone Fox.* New York: Harper & Row.

Hansen, J. (1992). *Which way freedom?* New York: Avon.

Harris, D. (1993). *Sweet Clara and the freedom quilt.* New York: Knopf.

Hoffman, M. (1991). *Amazing Grace.* London: Frances Lincoln.

Lowry, L. (1989). *Number the stars.* Boston: Houghton Mifflin.

Martin, B. (1967). *Brown bear, brown bear, what do you see?* New York: Henry Holt.

MacLachlan, P. (1985). *Sarah, plain and tall.* New York: Harper & Row.

Munsch, R., & Kusugak, M. (1989). *A promise is a promise.* Willowdale, Ontario: Firefly.

Paterson, K. (1972). *Bridge to Terabithia.* New York: Harper & Row.

Paulsen, G. (1987). *Hatchet.* New York: Bradbury Press.

Polacco, P. (1992). *Chicken Sunday.* New York: Philomel.

Ringgold, F. (1991). *Tar Beach.* New York: Crown.

Reeder, C. (1989). *Shades of gray.* New York: Macmillan.

Speare, E. G. (1958). *The witch of Blackbird Pond.* New York: Bantam Doubleday Dell.

Speare, E. G. (1983). *Sign of the beaver.* Boston: Dell.

Winter, J. (1988). *Follow the drinking gourd.* New York: Knopf.

▶ 5

Preparing for and Reacting to Change in Grouping Arrangements

**MARGUERITE C. RADENCICH and
LYN J. McKAY**

The importance of what we share here is not the grouping possibilities alone, but the underlying beliefs and assumptions which led us to their use. . . . They are not simply logistical mechanisms that can be plugged into any classroom. They are thoughtful choices of organizational patterns that support learning and the creating of meaning in the way we theorize it can best be accomplished. (Berghoff & Egawa, 1991)

Changing grouping arrangements can change the bedrock of the classroom. There's much, much more to preparing for change in grouping arrangements than meets the eye. Regie Routman (1991) mentions that the move away from homogeneous grouping in her classroom took ten years. Preparing for district change involves much time as well. Following is a graphic organizer of this chapter's information on district preparation for, and reaction to, change. Information for this chapter is culled from the Florida experience of Dade and Pinellas counties.

Preparing for Change in Grouping Arrangements

How Teachers and Administrators Need to Prepare

Examine any district barriers to change	Study budgets for instructional materials	Communicate with parents
Plan furniture arrangements	Think through lesson-plan formats	Plan how to conduct ongoing professional education

How to Conduct Ongoing Professional Education

Where to start	How to use support staff	How to provide models	How to carry out ongoing staff development

What Schools Should Expect

Initial uncertainty	Increased expectations for all students	Increased self-esteem and positive attitudes	Easier curricular integration
Teachers requesting sufficient materials	A growing understanding that all students can learn		Use of volunteers, paraprofessionals, and teachers in a new way
Changing classroom cultures		A number of concerns when implementing flexible grouping	

WHAT DO TEACHERS AND ADMINISTRATORS NEED TO DO?

Teachers and administrators must do a lot of communicating, simultaneously juggling attention on a number of issues when planning for changes in grouping arrangements:

- Examine any district barriers to the change.
- Study budgets for instructional materials.

- Communicate with parents.
- Plan furniture arrangements.
- Think through lesson-plan formats.
- Plan how to conduct ongoing professional education.

Examine Any District Barriers to the Change

District polices can inhibit change. Following are two examples. District requirements for basal unit tests will be problematic for teachers who base their instruction on trade books. A second example involves the mismatch that occurs when policies require that instruction be primarily at a tested instructional level when, in practice, teachers stretch students beyond this point. Thus, if all students are receiving some of their reading instruction with grade level material, problems may appear with report cards or special education referral forms that adhere to the district policy of instruction at the tested level. Perhaps the teacher must list reading level on the report card. In this case, does the teacher list tested level or level of materials in actual use? Perhaps the district requires that students not on grade level receive no grade higher than a "C." If so, how do teachers grade if they are teaching on grade level but they know their students really are not functioning at that level? The problem with special education referrals: There may be an expectation that the basic reading materials for students referred to gifted programs will be above level and those for candidates of learning disabilities classes will be below level, a situation which will not exist if all students are working primarily from grade level text.

District planning to use flexible grouping should examine any district policies that would interfere. Neglecting to do this up-front results in fitting the proverbial round pegs into square holes until district policies are aligned.

Study Budgets for Instructional Materials

A second area administrators and teachers should address in preparation for change into flexible grouping is equipping classrooms with enough appropriate materials. If all students are to read from common grade level basals or from the same trade books, budgets should be built to purchase books for all children or at least for every pair of children. This may mean reallocating funds to equip classrooms with enough copies of books for whole-class reading, rather than the stratified purchasing that has been done to accommodate a three-group reading program (Paratore, 1991).

It is also essential that classroom libraries provide a range of easy and challenging texts for self-selected and teacher-directed extended reading. Group sets of four to six copies of some titles can be most helpful, particularly in the case of predictable books (e.g., Rigby and Wright Group series) for emergent readers, or other relatively easy titles for older students who are not yet proficient readers. Classroom libraries should go well beyond the libraries basal publishers sell to supplement their reading programs; they should be varied and include at least three to five books per student. In the words of one second-grade teacher, "I need at least one hundred books so my struggling students can practice reading at their own level."

Communicate with Parents

A third area requiring preparation is planning for efficient communication with parents. In our districts, flexible grouping initially took the form of teaching all students from a common basal grade level selection, with use of additional materials both below and above this level. We were surprised at the smoothness with which our parents accepted flexible grouping. Most parents expressed support for what many of them said "makes sense." Problems occurred, though, where teachers were dissatisfied and conveyed their dissatisfaction to parents. In anticipation of parent questions and concerns, Pinellas County supervisors spoke about flexible grouping at approximately thirty-five PTA meetings. This was close to half the schools in the district. In Dade County, schools wishing to explain the change to parents either used school staff for this purpose or invited district staff or basal company representatives to speak at morning or evening PTA meetings.

Parents' questions related primarily to how much opportunity there would be each day for students to interact directly with the teacher. A few parents of the highly skilled readers were concerned about their children being challenged. Most were pleased to learn their children would have an opportunity on a daily basis to read in materials on their reading level. They were told students would have a chance to choose books of interest to them. Supervisors also pointed out that flexible-group instruction from grade-appropriate text could even be richer than what their children were receiving previously. One principal persuaded parents by showing them side-by-side selections from trade books and edited selections from a traditional basal with controlled vocabulary, controlled length and choice of selections, and sentences of limited length and type.

In responding to parents' concerns, it is also important to explain that text levels are not the only or the optimal way to challenge or provide extra help; rather, teachers will rely more on different strategies than on different texts (Paratore, 1991). The situation with parents of high achievers must be handled with particular tact if the students had previously been in a high group and parents or students object to losing this prestige. Prestige may also be found in other ways, such as careful use of high achievers as peer tutors and opportunities to excel with extended projects.

We have found parents of low achievers to be generally pleased with the higher expectations, as long as they see their children's needs will be met. Often, they have been vocal in their praise of flexible grouping, finding major improvement in the attitudes of their children—not just toward reading, but toward school as a whole. Parents of average children need to be reassured, too, that their children will not be slighted. If, after whole-class instruction, teacher-facilitated needs-based groups are pulled, these groups will most likely be high or low achievers requiring special directions. Parents accustomed to seeing their average children receive one-third of the instructional time in an ability group will need to be shown that all children will have some small-group instruction, and that their children are not being neglected.

We know of one high socioeconomic school in which parents were impressed following a show and tell assembly early in the school year. Students proudly showed off challenging projects they had completed in class. Other "PR" options include a telecast or a mailing directed to parents. A sample parent mailing follows in Figure 5-1.

FIGURE 5-1   Sample Parent Mailing

Reading

What Is New?
During the 1990–1991 school year, students in kindergarten through fifth grade will embark on a new journey into literacy when Pinellas County begins using the Health Reading program in conjunction with a flexible-grouping model for instruction. The goals of this program are to nurture children's love for reading and to provide the skills and strategies necessary to be effective life-long readers.

The Heath Reading series your child will be using will help create an excitement for reading. Students will be learning strategies that will help them in and out of the classroom, working with other students, doing projects, and reading more than ever. Be prepared for trips to the library!

Children will also be writing more than ever and will probably see themselves as important authors of their very own books and books their class will write as a group. Their writings will, in many cases, be related directly to the reading they are doing. Please have a supply of paper and pencils on hand at home. You never know when your budding author will get a great idea!

Elementary reading and language arts teachers will be using a different grouping model for the teaching of reading. The model is known as flexible grouping, and in it all students in the classroom begin with the same reading selection. Then children have daily opportunities to practice reading books and stories on their individual reading levels.

This flexible-grouping model has been tried successfully in Pinellas County since November, 1989, by 12 first-grade teachers and 12 fourth-grade teachers. Overall, 88% of Pinellas classroom teachers and administrators, grades K–5, voted to implement the model countywide.

FIGURE 5-1 *(Continued)*

We are learning more and more these days about how children learn to read and what makes them good readers. Current research supports the introduction of phonics in the early grades and indicates that a strong emphasis on the meaning of a passage creates better readers. The Heath Reading materials include both phonics and an emphasis on comprehension.

The research findings also support the use of the flexible-grouping model, which involves grouping children in a variety of ways rather than keeping the same reading groups throughout the year. For example, children may work with a partner, in a small group, or with the whole class. The basis for grouping may be students' instructional level, skill needs, or interest in a particular topic or author.

We believe that the exciting literature found in Heath Reading and the learning opportunities for students using the flexible-grouping model will make a winning combination! With your support and involvement, 1990–1991 will be a most successful year.

What Can You Expect?

- An emphasis on literature by authors and artists children love such as Marc Brown, James Marshall, and Tomie de Paola
- Writing, speaking, and listening activities connected to the literature in the reading program
- Reading skill instruction, including phonics, connected to the literature in the reading program
- An emphasis on learning strategies that empower students to read and think on their own
- Exciting projects that promote cooperate learning and enhance reading
- Use of technology to create a stimulating environment for reading

Source: Reprinted with permission from Pinellas County Schools.

Plan Furniture Arrangements

Whatever the size of the classroom, administrators and teachers should plan furniture arrangement with their grouping structures in mind. We know of teachers who have decided that less is better and have removed desks to make room for tables and centers. Many teachers seat heterogeneous groups of students together to allow for easy peer tutoring, buddy reading, and cooperative learning. Teachers planning to use cooperative learning may want areas students will move to when they work with groups. Or, group members may be assigned adjoining seats for a period of time. One sixth-grade teacher periodically moved students into different seating groups. Their first chore as a new group would be to draw a sign to hang over their desks. This helped the group begin to bond immediately. Optimally, furniture arrangements should allow for whole-class, small-group, and individual instruction.

Think Through Lesson Plan Formats*

How does flexible grouping fit into lesson plans? This will be a major issue for many administrators and teachers to consider during their planning and initial implementation of flexible grouping. Lesson plans have traditionally fit into nice, neat little boxes: boxes for each day of the week, for each subject area, for each reading group. These plan formats just do not work for flexible-group instruction. We have seen teachers struggle with a number of alternatives. Lesson plans are so personal that no single alternative works for everyone. Following are sections which address the issues of lesson-plan components and alternatives.

Components of Lesson Plans.   Aside from problems with the traditional lesson-plan components (e.g., which objectives do you list when you're probably covering quite a few?), there are lesson-plan questions that directly relate to flexible grouping. These include decisions on whether/how to distinguish between (a) whole-class activities and (b) group activities that are teacher- or student-directed.

Lesson Plan Alternatives

→ **1. Pinellas County Public Schools Model.** Most Pinellas County teachers use a lesson planner designed by a committee to help organize reading and language arts instruction according to Pinellas' four circle model of flexible grouping (see Chapter 3). After the first year, teachers simplified the model. Following are the models used in Year 1 and Year 2.

Figure 5-2 is a reproduction of the lesson planner used the first year of implementation. It has space for each of the four core activities in the flexible-grouping model: reading-selection instruction, writing, self-selected reading, and skill and strategy instruction. It also has space for planning enrichment activities.

Figure 5-3 is a reproduction of the simplified lesson planner teachers designed after a year's experience using flexible grouping.

A few teachers continue to use a standard plan book. Some have put their plans on computer. Whatever plan form they use, they incorporate all four elements of the Pinellas flexible-grouping model.

---

*Adapted from M. C. Radencich, "Integrated Lesson Plan Formats: How Do You Fit It All In?" *Florida Reading Quarterly*, Vol. 29, No. 2, 1992, pp. 15–17.

Teacher _____

For the week of _____

Scheduling Information	Reading Selection Instruction — Preparing to Read / Reading and Rereading (Silent and Oral) / Discussion / Skill Instruction	Writing — Writing Sharing Daily	Self-Selected Reading — Reading Sharing Daily	Skill and Strategy Instruction — Skill or Strategy Reinforcement in Context of Reading	Enrichment Activities: Read Aloud	Applying Ideas and/or Content Area	Centers and/or Project	Spelling, Language, Handwriting
Monday / Lesson # ___	Gps	Gps	Gps	Gps				
Tuesday / Lesson # ___	Gps	Gps	Gps	Gps				
Wednesday / Lesson # ___	Gps	Gps	Gps	Gps				
Thursday / Lesson # ___	Gps	Gps	Gps	Gps				
Friday / Lesson # ___	Gps	Gps	Gps	Gps				

FIGURE 5-2 Pinellas County Lesson Planner, Year 1

Source: Reprinted with permission from Pinellas County Schools.

Teacher _____

Week of _____

Scheduling Information	Reading Selection Instruction — Preparing to Read, Reading and Rereading (Silent and Oral) Discussion Skill Instruction	Writing — Writing Sharing Daily	Self-Selected Reading — Reading Sharing Daily	Skill and Strategy Instruction — Skill or Strategy Reinforcement in Context of Reading
Monday				
Tuesday				
Wednesday				
Thursday				
Friday				

FIGURE 5-3 Pinellas County Lesson Planner, Year 2

Source: Reprinted with permission from Pinellas County Schools.

━━➤ **2. Dade County Public Schools Model.** With the implementation of flexible grouping in Dade County, the reading staff developed a repertoire of sample lesson-plan formats with varying degrees of structure, knowing that some teachers would want to start with a "cookbook," and others would be ready for more open-ended formats. Lesson plans for sample selections were written to model form use. Alternative teacher-made formats were later collected and distributed. Some sample forms are provided in Figure 5-4.

The result? Some teachers continued with traditional formats although they had switched to more integrated and flexible instruction. Others used new formats but did not change traditional instructional procedures. Still others did show congruence between what was on paper and what actually took place in the classroom. Some teachers annotated the most detailed format or used it in addition to plans they typed or wrote longhand. Some, unfortunately, used the detailed format only as a checklist.

━━➤ **3. Clusters.** Another lesson-plan model: cluster plans, or webs resembling the spokes on a wheel. The center is a theme or a common selection, surrounded by activities grouped as desired by the teacher (e.g., related readings, vocabulary words, content connections, writing, centers). We have seen kindergarten and first-grade teachers use daily clusters of the activities they plan around the Big Book of the day. Theme clusters on posterboards can help the whole class see where they are going. These can be easier to fill out than clusters on paper since the teacher does not have to spend time figuring out how to condense everything. An alternative to posterboards could be magnetic boards with movable pieces (student names, activity choices, etc.) serving to organize flexible grouping.

Cluster planning can be intimidating for some teachers. But for those who are interested, questions to ask include:

- Will the clustering be for all instruction, or only for reading and language arts?
- Will the cluster stand alone or will it be a skeleton accompanied later by more detailed plans?
- Will clustering be by day or for the duration of a theme?
- Will the cluster be organized into subject areas? Or would this still look too much like traditional squares in a plan book?

A class of graduate students asked to cluster plans for a week all chose to put in the center the theme and/or the selection title(s), some inside an attractive theme-related illustration. One student clustered by day, with five circles around the theme; the procedures were the main circles, with orbiting circles for each day's objectives, materials, and evaluation. A pair of students working together chose the following organization around a theme: introduction, applying ideas, skills and strategies, language activities, and theme project; attached were detailed daily plans in an outline format.

FIGURE 5-4   Dade County Sample Lesson-Plan Formats

Source: Reprinted with permission from Dade County Public Schools.

Another graduate student's titles were: purpose, reading, writing projects, spelling/vocabulary, handwriting, content area, home discovery projects. This student then had a color-coded key clarifying the days when each activity would take place, and the form of evaluation for each. She also had a clever revolving centerpiece that celebrated her instructional philosophy. See Figure 5-5 for portions of the plan.

A final pair of graduate students coded each activity as to teacher direction, student participation, day of delivery, and sequence within each day. They used the following structure: student reading time, video/read-aloud, cross-curricular activities, skills and strategies, language activities, evaluations. Most of these sections were accompanied by a speech balloon with a list of objectives.

If clustering can help children organize their writing, maybe it can help teachers organize their writing of lesson plans as well.

⟶ 4. Use of Technology. Other lesson-plan models capitalize on the availability of current technology. Some teachers use word processors to easily copy or change lesson-plan items from one week to the next. This might be a combination of outline and paragraph formats. The objectives and materials for an entire selection can be listed on Day 1. Flexible-grouping activities and evaluations can be simply explained for each day.

If teachers want to use technology beyond word processing, and see information organized in more than one way (e.g., by objective, by day of the week, by subject area), a database could be ideal, especially if all teachers and administrators at a school use the same database. One teacher might print the information by day and the administrator might look at it by day as well as by objective.

Another intriguing option is the use of software specifically designed for lesson planning. Three programs in this category are Teaching's *Plan to Teach* (1990), *Planit* from Amberon (1990), and Apple Computer's *Educator Home Card* (1990), all available for both the IBM and the MacIntosh, and all requiring a hard drive.

- **Plan to Teach** allows for the creation of four types of plans: weekly plans, daily plans, individual lesson plans, and a skills checklist. The program includes samples of each. The formats are similar to those found in many lesson-plan books. They can be customized.
- **Planit** is a HyperCard program designed to integrate planning, classroom scheduling, and curriculum implementation. Its modules include Day Book, Plans, Calendar, and Resources. A master schedule is created. Timetables can be set on daily, weekly, or other cyclical schedules. High-quality graphics are an additional enhancement.

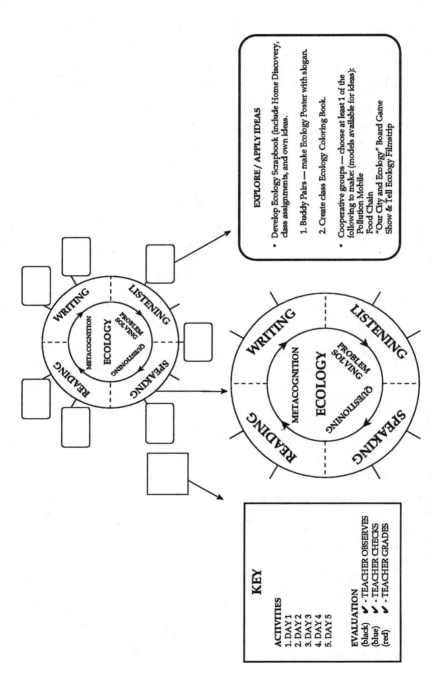

FIGURE 5-5 One Cluster Lesson-Plan Alternative

EXPLORE / APPLY IDEAS

• Develop Ecology Scrapbook (include Home Discovery, class assignments, and own ideas.

1. Buddy Pairs — make Ecology Poster with slogan.

2. Create class Ecology Coloring Book.

• Cooperative groups — choose at least 1 of the following to make: (models available for ideas);
Pollution Mobile
Food Chain
"Our City and Ecology" Board Game
Show & Tell Ecology Filmstrip

WRITING LISTENING READING SPEAKING
METACOGNITION PROBLEM SOLVING QUESTIONING ECOLOGY

KEY

ACTIVITIES
1. DAY 1
2. DAY 2
3. DAY 3
4. DAY 4
5. DAY 5

EVALUATION
(black) ✔ - TEACHER OBSERVES
(blue) ✔ - TEACHER CHECKS
(red) ✔ - TEACHER GRADES

- **Education HomeCard** is a set of HyperCard stacks that provides Student Management tools and Lesson Management tools (Calendar, Lesson Plans, and Presentation Stack). The program creates a card for each lesson plan, which has space to enter objectives, additional resources, preparation information, activities, and evaluation. Teachers can elect from a list of key words to find related lessons. Lesson-plan titles can be transferred to a Planner Calendar. Sample lesson plans are included. This product makes use of HyperCard 2.0 capabilities such as animation and sound.

Use of computers for lesson plans is a possibility all teachers might consider, even if only the simpler word-processing and database options are used.

➤ **5. Logs.** Still another lesson-plan model is the use of lesson-plan books or notebooks with several blank lines per day. This simplicity parallels the blank page on which students write in whole language classrooms. In one school that uses such a plan, teachers are only required to note what they would do and what the anticipated result would be.

Regardless of the option used, the lesson plan need not always be the exclusive responsibility of the teacher. With individualized programs, it is possible for students to do at least some of the recording of their own lesson plans. We know of one case where a teacher empowered her students to take this responsibility. Even more important than the reduction in her paper work, she found student involvement helped with student ownership as well.

A frequently asked question is how to handle lesson plans for substitutes. If the structure is too difficult for a substitute teacher to handle, we frequently suggest replacing regular plans with simpler emergency plans for use when the need arises.

Changes in teaching may well require changes in lesson-plan formats. Time should be spent choosing a possible format, with opportunities for reevaluating and changing this form as needed.

Thus far, this chapter has dealt with how teachers and administrators need to prepare for change in grouping arrangements. The next section addresses ongoing professional education as grouping arrangements are changed. The final section of the chapter deals with what schools should expect from this process.

Plan How to Conduct
Ongoing Professional Education

As with any instructional change, shifting grouping patterns requires opportunities for teachers to explore the theoretical literature, to learn from colleagues, and to share their own ideas and experiences. Such exploration is likely to be far more effective when groups of teachers collaborate in this process than when teachers embark on it alone. Thus, providing a forum for discussion, through regularly scheduled and planned meetings, is highly recommended (Paratore, 1991). Staff development issues that follow are: where to start, use of support staff, provision of models, and means of carrying out ongoing staff development.

Where to Start.   Starting with a pilot group is sometimes feasible. As with any changes that directly affect teaching and learning, teachers often feel the most secure when they can hear from other teachers who have tried an innovation. Time can be well spent when a group of teachers, supervisors, and administrators work together to pilot flexible grouping. It is important that any pilot last a sufficient amount of time for teachers to explore options and discuss their activities on a regular basis. A yearlong pilot is ideal. The time spent in piloting will prevent problems and save time when others implement flexible grouping later.

An example of a pilot is an eight-month Pinellas County, Florida, study in which twelve Grade 1 teachers and twelve Grade 4 teachers, one from each of twenty-four schools, volunteered to try a flexible-grouping model with one of the six basal series Pinellas County was considering for adoption. Teachers met as a group at least one afternoon each month with the district reading/language arts supervisors. The district was advised by Patricia M. Cunningham from Wake Forest University and by Jeanne R. Paratore from Boston University regarding their experiences with flexible-grouping models. Near the end of the year, the trial-use teachers held after-school meetings for the hundreds of teachers who wanted to learn about the flexible-grouping program. Every elementary administrator and reading and language arts teacher was then given an opportunity to vote on countywide use of flexible grouping. A remarkable 90% returned the ballots. Those responding voted overwhelmingly (83%) in favor of implementation. After formal approval from a committee of twenty-two teachers, administrators, and parents, preparation for implementation began.

If a district elects not to begin with a pilot, staff development for all teachers and administrators should optimally begin before program implementation. It is important to try to convey the impact a change in grouping will have on overall classroom organization. At the same time, it is important not to overwhelm school staffs. A 2-year staff development plan is a minimum starting point if the implementation is to be reasonably smooth. Districts should work with schools in selecting priority areas within the issues related to flexible grouping. It also may not be possible to carry out other inservice initiatives while staffs are beginning to deal with flexible grouping.

Teachers starting to implement heterogeneous grouping may find it easier to commit to try just for one selection, for one month, or for one summer. The first selections tried should be easy enough for teachers and students to comfortably explore the new methods without being too challenged with the content. Teachers may start with one type of flexible group, and gradually add others.

How to Use Support Staff.   Support staff such as curriculum specialists, media specialists, paraprofessionals, and volunteers should be included in staff development plans early on. We have found that inservice sessions by media specialists or by special education teachers for their peers are optimal ways of involving these support staff.

In the case of media specialists, sessions can include the need for rotating collections of multilevel materials related to the themes teachers are using in their classrooms. Another need is providing open library times for use by ad hoc groups that are perhaps working on a project or have left the classroom because they do not need to listen to a read-aloud of the common selection.

Volunteers and paraprofessionals are other support staff who can help with flexible grouping, both outside of and within the classroom setting. With flexible grouping, teachers continually juggle their schedules to try to meet student needs. Properly trained volunteers and paraprofessionals can help alleviate scheduling problems by working with small flexible groups or individuals.

How to Provide Models.   As with any change, one staff development option schools often request is models. This is a ticklish issue with flexible grouping, an art exercised differently by each individual teacher. But this is precisely why models can be helpful. Thus, models appear often in the following staff development options:

⟶ **1. Interschool Visitations.** The district can compile a list of teachers who are comfortable with their implementation to encourage inter- or intraschool visitations. Following are some pointers for success:

• Visits should be made to situations similar to those of the visitors. It is easier, for example, for a teacher of limited English proficient, lower socioeconomic students to learn from a teacher with a similar class than to learn from a teacher of a different population.

- If possible, administrators and teachers should visit during instructional periods.
- Visits should be made to more than one classroom to show there is no one right way.
- Teachers should go in groups of at least two, possibly with a weaker and a stronger teacher making visits together.
- Visits work best when preceded by previsitation discussions to prepare visitors for what to look for.
- Visits should be followed up with discussions about what might be used among the options observed.

➤ **2. School Contact Person.**   A second option for the use of models is the appointment of a school contact person who shares information, models lessons, and otherwise coaches peers. Coaching (Joyce & Showers, 1982) has been shown to be invaluable for true change. A curriculum specialist, or perhaps one intermediate and one primary teacher, can attend district level meetings, communicate as needed with district staff, and then provide support. Sharing generally does not take place, however, if the contact teacher does not have time set aside for this purpose.

➤ **3. Demonstrations by District Personnel.**   A third type of models, demonstrations on the part of district personnel or others, might take different forms:

- Teachers can move through simulated flexible groups and learning centers.
- Procedures can be set up for actual classroom demonstrations. Dade County coordinators found the need to initiate a four-step procedure to ensure greater understanding and dissemination: (a) several teachers are released to sit in, (b) the presenter prepares plans for the lesson and makes sure that teachers have copies of these as well as teachers' manuals if appropriate, (c) an administrator joins the group, and (d) there is time scheduled for discussion at a follow-up session.
- Classroom demonstrations can be videotaped. We hear constant requests for videotape models. This is not as simple as it sounds. Should any videotaping include all grade levels? Some teachers find it hard to generalize from grade levels other than their own. Should there be more than one teacher per grade level to show diverse ways of implementing flexible grouping? Which portions of the instruction are to be taped? An entire instructional sequence, which might take place over several days, would make a tape unwieldy. Districts might not have the resources for the kind of editing necessary to adequately respond to all these issues with a tape of reasonable length. An ideal solution where possible would be compressing videotapes into a videodisc with viewers having ready access to any footage of interest. A more modest option tried in Dade County with some success was that of a staged lesson. The supervisor

visits a teacher to plan a multiday lesson, carrying out Day 1 while getting to know the students, inviting visitors and videotaping the lesson on Day 2, and leaving plans for the classroom teacher to use/adapt on remaining days.

Dade County has also used three commercial 15-minute Houghton Mifflin tapes, each of which show a sample of teachers from a given grade range using flexible grouping with trade books. This has been of limited success, however, because commercial tapes tend to be seen as canned and not realistic in terms of class size and class population. Pinellas County has used a tape made in the district by Heath. It shows Pinellas County's flexible-grouping model in a Grade 1 and a Grade 3 classroom. It was well received by Pinellas County teachers, probably in part because it was made in their own district.

Rather than select one of the above types of models, a combination of approaches will probably be best to meet the needs of most local situations.

How to Carry Out Ongoing School Level Staff Staff Development

Schools will find new questions and problems arise as they spend time using flexible-grouping models. Thus, staff development must be ongoing, probably changing from whole-faculty instruction in the beginning to more individualized support later on. In addition to participating in the staff development efforts discussed already, school administrators might exercise some of the following options:

➤ **1.** Allocate a substantial portion of regularly scheduled faculty or grade level meetings for issues relating to flexible grouping. This might include sharing, discussion of articles on the subject, or use of guest speakers.

➤ **2.** Explore reasonable options with teachers for staff development where none seem to exist. In one school teachers suggested a series of breakfast meetings to be held before school to explore a specific issue and share experiences. In another, teachers chose to meet monthly after school for 45-minute open agenda meetings to resolve difficulties and share successes (Paratore, 1991).

➤ **3.** Conduct an in-house program review in which teachers agree on an evaluating instrument, evaluation procedures, and the fellow teachers who will visit the classrooms. Recommendations are made for each grade level or for the school as a whole, not for individual teachers.

➤ **4.** Assign buddies to new teachers. Optimally, the buddies could be together for several days, or for an entire instructional sequence.

➤ **5.** Set up study groups. In Year 2, Dade County set up study-group sessions with administrators (Radencich, 1993). A flyer announcing a four-morning set of seminars—with readings to do before each session, and with a request that a response log be kept too—resulted in a list of 68 participants in only two days. The four topics were whole language, flexible grouping, assessment, and writing. The hunger for information and for networking opportunities was real. Most of the selected readings were of a practical bent, such as the teacher success stories told by Richek and Glick (1991) and Cunningham (1991), but Dade County did not shy away from including a few heavier pieces such as Hiebert (1991) to round out historical background. Humorous and poignant pieces were used as well.

➤ **6.** Use resources beyond the school district. Local reading councils or TAWL (Teachers Approaching Whole Language) groups may be able to schedule question-and-answer and sharing sessions for teachers by grade level. Local, state, and national professional organizations provide helpful publications and conferences. Support can also be enlisted from local universities. After the onset of flexible grouping in Dade County, one professor videotaped a district inservice session for school administrators, edited the tape, and made it available to the local universities. One meeting of the Florida Organization of Teacher Educators in Reading included a round table for district supervisors to discuss current district initiatives with interested teacher educators, including flexible grouping.

➤ **7.** Help teachers find more time for working with various types of groups as they become more flexible themselves:

- Learn to juggle schedules creatively by crossing subject boundaries and working with one group while others work on tasks not requiring teacher assistance. The teacher might, for example, find time for a group by sometimes giving up modeling silent reading or journal writing, or by assigning some students to learning centers, handwriting, or mathematics practice.
- Become more comfortable releasing responsibility to students in cooperative groups, peer tutoring situations, and individual activities.
- Decrease the use of isolated materials such as workbooks and spelling and English books.

- Become comfortable with differentiating instruction; not all students need to experience the same learning activities.
- Begin to grade students differentially. There may not be time for students pulled for an ad hoc group to complete a story sequel, or the difficulty level of that task may not be appropriate for some students.

This section has addressed ongoing professional education. Change is hard enough even when there are professional education opportunities. Without this support, it is often doomed to failure. Schools are encouraged to work together, remembering the three "T's" in Things Take Time.

WHAT SHOULD SCHOOLS EXPECT?

Following the implementation of flexible grouping, schools should expect some frustration but, eventually, great satisfaction. As administrators and teachers retrain students, parents, and themselves, they must be patient. It *will* be hard work. But schools will be rewarded when visitors have trouble telling the high achievers from the less skilled students. Following are some specific answers to what schools should expect.

Initial Uncertainty

During the first year of transition to flexible grouping, we, as supervisors, were not always sure what we were seeing in classrooms. Each classroom took on its own look, and what may have appeared to be lack of organization, because traditional reading groups were not evident, may have been well-planned flexible grouping. In classrooms where teachers were comfortable with flexible grouping and were differentiating instruction, there was obviously more reading and writing going on. These teachers spent more time interacting with individuals and groups of students, and the students spent more time engaged in authentic, purposeful reading and writing activities. In classrooms where teachers had given up traditional grouping but had not yet learned to manage flexible grouping, we saw a lot of whole-group instruction and frequent paired reading but few small-group meetings with the teacher.

Increased Expectations for All Students

The increased expectations—and achievement—for all students may not be immediate but, if everything is in place, it will happen. First-grade teachers, who feel responsible to turn nonreaders into readers, can be particularly nervous in the interim. Some teachers realize several months into the implementation that *It works!* These teachers have managed to find a balance between whole-group and small-group instruction, and have changed members of their groups frequently. Following is one teacher's view:

> *"I've seen a lot of progress. By hearing the story from me and then some choral reading and retelling . . . I've seen their scores go up. Some ESOL students are doing better than some of the kids who have been here all the time. They're really listening."*—DOROTHY MORDICA, Grade 4 teacher

The increased expectations must be transmitted to parents, assertively if necessary:

> *"My lowest students couldn't read at all. Their parents are really helping. One is reading all the time. He reads at home. He reads and comprehends."*
> —BARBARA VICTOR, Grade 3 teacher

Increased Self-Esteem and Positive Attitudes

Low achieving youngsters who are allowed for the first time to work with higher achievers are sometimes so pleased they rise to the occasion. As well as changing how students see themselves, heterogeneous grouping affects how students view others. A flexible-grouping model permits students to observe that their peers bring a range of strengths and needs to a task, with different students being better at different skills such as reading, writing, drawing, and organizing (Paratore, 1991). One Grade 4 teacher commented, "My fast students know we are all at different levels of reading and should help one another. There isn't as much competition now."

Easier Integration of the Curriculum

Flexible grouping provides the framework for high and low achievers to work with writing that stems from shared selections or themes. Teachers who are trying to integrate the entire curriculum may find more planning and instructional time when subject-area boundaries are diffuse and theme-based teaching takes place in large time blocks. They may find more opportunities for needs-based groups and individual teaching as well as the more traditional content area instruction in whole groups. Teachers replacing traditional ability groups with classwide thematic instruction will also find more time for activities relating to *one* theme than to three themes from three ability groups. Schools will probably see a decrease in the use of spelling, language arts, and handwriting books in favor of more writing in response to reading.

Teachers Requesting Sufficient Materials for Self-Selected and Teacher-Directed Reading

As was alluded to early in the chapter, a wealth of trade books and magazines is needed either as a supplement or as the core of instruction. Great variety is needed to challenge and help high and low achieving students. Book drives can be especially effective in lower grades, since parents of higher grade students may have books at home their children will have outgrown. We know of one teacher who let it be known that if parents were going to buy her Christmas presents, she wanted nothing but children's books for her classroom. Parents can donate a book to the school library on their child's birthday, with a nameplate recognizing the donation. Children-authored books should abound in classroom and school libraries. Books can be bought for next to nothing at garage sales, used book stores, and flea markets; extra discounts can even be obtained when the purpose for the purchase is explained. Collections in classrooms can be rotated to other rooms. Monies normally spent on workbooks or in other areas can often be rerouted. Support can be enlisted from local businesses. Means for building adequate collections must be found if flexible grouping is to meet the needs of all students.

A Growing Understanding That All Students Can Learn

Schools implementing flexible grouping should foster a growing understanding that all students can learn but may not master all material taught at the same rate. This is an important understanding. Some children will not learn all the words, all the skills, all the concepts on the same day. Because of differential learning rates, accelerated instruction may be necessary for some students. An understanding that materials need not be followed blindly, that reading is not necessarily learned sequentially (Hiebert, 1987), and that skills will recycle helps teachers become flexible in their decisions.

Use of Volunteers, Paraprofessionals, and Special Teachers in New Ways

As mentioned previously, flexible grouping is resulting in changing roles of volunteers, paraprofessionals, and special teachers. Properly trained volunteers are beginning to spend more time working with small groups. In several schools, for example, teachers have created kits for volunteers to use to assist struggling readers. These kits include a specific instructional sequence for using short predictable texts, instructions for increasing phonemic awareness, and suggestions for ways to help students partner read or echo read.

Paraprofessionals and special teachers are spending more time with in-class models. Traditionally, teachers could meet with a low group before or after those students were pulled out for additional help. With flexible grouping, students' groups and activities are continually changing. It is more difficult to establish a consistent time each day when pull-out students are not working directly with the classroom teacher.

Some schools are training paraprofessionals through the Chapter 1 program to assist with flexible grouping in teachers' classrooms. In the past, teachers often have resisted having support teachers and/or paraprofessionals in their classrooms in our districts. However, when both the classroom teacher and the assisting volunteer, paraprofessional, or special teacher know the specific learner outcomes intended and a flexible-grouping model is in place, teachers appear more open to the concept of an in-class support model. When students are pulled out in Dade County, teachers have found the need for a different kind of articulation than was previously necessary. In place of a list of skills, the Chapter 1 form consists of a series of activities that support a flexible-grouping plan (see Figure 5-6). Note the inclusion of an early bird plan in Figure 5-6. This use of Chapter 1 personnel before classroom instruction is a departure from traditional models where Chapter 1 instruction is delivered only after a teacher's introduction of the material.

The use of paraprofessionals, volunteers, and Chapter 1 personnel is not the only area where support roles are changing. Special education is too. Special education teachers have always had difficulty organizing instruction if they are faced with revolving-door schedules with students of widely disparate levels from different grade classrooms. If students receive all their reading and language arts instruction in a special class, the problem is easier to address, as the special education teacher can elect to teach the group from a grade-appropriate trade book, or to move toward a reading workshop model (Atwell, 1987) with thematically related materials of different levels. In one more traditional school large enough to have two special education teachers, the two teachers regrouped their students by reading level rather than grade level as they had previously. They then each taught from two levels of books, stretching students to one or the other level.

If the regular and special education teachers share responsibility for reading and language arts, the difficulty of coordinating instruction is more severe, especially if they are trying to cross curricular boundaries. Schedules might be changed to an in-class inclusion model, where the special education teacher facilitates flexible grouping, focusing on special education students in their regular class, either alone or in small groups. The downside here is that the special education students must be segregated into a limited number of regular classrooms if the special education teacher is to spend a meaningful length of time in each.

Dade County Public Schools
Chapter 1 Program Reading Articulation Form

SCHOOL _____ WEEK OF: _____

			SUGGESTED ACTIVITIES #1						ADDITIONAL ACTIVITIES								
Classroom Teacher	Chapter 1 Paraprofessional	Chapter 1 Teacher	STUDENTS	With guided assistance the pupil will:	Listen to a reading of the core/basal selection; current ____ next ____	Listen to a selection; view film/pictures: related to current selection/theme ____ pupil's choice ____	Reread core/basal selection pages: first and last ____; pupil selected ____ teacher selected ____	Read instructional level mini-books	Retell core/basal selection ____; complete story map ____; compose questions ____								
			1.														
			2.														
			3.														
			4.														
			5.														
			6.														
			7.														
			8.														

COMMENTS AND-OR RECOMMENDATIONS (Include date (s) of comments):

FIGURE 5-6 Chapter 1 Articulation Form

Dade County Public Schools
Chapter 1 Program Reading Articulation Form

SCHOOL _____ WEEK OF: _____

Classroom Teacher[a]
Chapter 1 Paraprofessional
Chapter 1 Teacher

STUDENTS	SUGGESTED ACTIVITIES #2								ADDITIONAL ACTIVITIES			
	With guided assistance a pupil will: Explain worksheet	Prepare for reading a library book to a group	Construct/play phonics puzzles — games — tongue twisters —	Apply comprehension strategies: complete frames —, games —, graphic organizers —, etc for —	Share writing: journal — other —	Use sight: —/core selection —; words to construct/play puzzles/games	Apply vocabulary (antonyms/synonyms, multiple meanings, etc.) strategies: maintain vocabulary notebook, write concrete, cinquain, etc. poetry; do word plays —	Engage in a writing conference to: read own piece — have assistance with revision: content — editing — [b]				
1.												
2.												
3.												
4.												
5.												
6.												
7.												
8.												

COMMENTS AND-OR RECOMMENDATIONS (Include date [s] of comments):

[a]Classroom teacher will indicate activities needed by a check (✓) or identify additional activities needed for reinforcement.
[b]Teacher-assisted activity.

FIGURE 5-6 (Continued)

Source: Reprinted with permission from Dade County Public Schools.

Another possibility we have seen work is to pair willing regular and special education teachers to team-teach a class with about half of the students being special education students. This can be accomplished in a school where there is a second special education teacher to handle the other grade levels. This model could be used in a school where there are not large numbers of special education students at any grade level with a combination or a multigrade class.

Allowing flexibility in the use of paraprofessionals, volunteers, and Chapter 1 and special education personnel can greatly enhance the effectiveness of flexible grouping.

Changing Classroom Cultures

In classrooms and schools where teachers are becoming comfortable with differentiating instruction and are managing a variety of grouping arrangements, a cultural change is occurring. We observe a spirit of cooperation and risk-taking. Some teachers are moving away from the mode of teaching that Jane Hansen (1987, p. 85) wrote "conveys to students that their knowledge is not important enough to share, that we [teachers] revere our own knowledge and transmit it, even though we know that this is not the way to accomplish the best learning." We are beginning to see some teachers take on a more facilitative role as they help students become a community of learners who are assuming more responsibility for their own learning than in the past. There is more evidence of cooperative work, including buddy reading, plays, and readers theater. Teachers are also expressing a need to find alternatives to criterion-referenced assessments and are looking for reporting procedures that reflect an integrated curriculum.

Not only are teaching and learning practices beginning to change in flexibly-grouped classrooms, the classroom itself is beginning to look different. Teachers and students are creating literate environments that have more student work displayed and many more classroom library books available. In many classrooms integrated projects are displayed. In some classrooms, furniture is removed to allow room for learning centers or beanbag chairs.

A Number of Concerns When Implementing Flexible Grouping

Schools should not expect that all will work smoothly in the implementation of flexible grouping. Although we were encouraged after even the first year by the enthusiasm of teachers, students, and parents, we and the teachers had some concerns. Some were logistical, some philosophical—such as the not-yet-solid understanding of the theory behind this change. The concerns are all closely interrelated.

→ **1. Overuse of Whole-Group Instruction.** The single most serious concern is the excessive use of whole-group instruction. Some teachers, particularly those using basal series, found themselves spending too much time in whole-group instruction in an effort to teach it all. They had not yet begun to change instruction sufficiently to accommodate the varying abilities of all of their students. In some first- and second-grade classes, for example, teachers, in an effort to conscientiously follow basal reader instructions, taught vocabulary using the same individual vocabulary cards for the total group. Some students benefitted from the activity, some already knew the vocabulary, and others had such severe difficulty reading the words that the activity was of little value. Teachers saw the problem but were still struggling with scheduling a variety of groups.

→ **2. Misunderstandings About the Acceptability of Using Needs-Based Groups for Less Proficient Readers.** Some teachers interpreted criticism of traditional ability grouping to mean that they should have no grouping by performance level, even on a temporary basis. Thus, they were not meeting with any small groups with specific needs. Some of the struggling students appeared to be missing planned instruction appropriate to their reading proficiency.

→ **3. Lack of Challenge for High Achievers.** As an extension of the problem with excessive whole-class instruction, high achievers were often not being adequately challenged to extend their knowledge both in groups and individually. The discussion, extended writing, and cooperative group activities related to the grade-appropriate text give an opportunity to expand learning. High achievers should be challenged through cooperative projects related to the theme or the author of a common selection, and through higher demands made on their oral and written contributions. Use of a grade-appropriate text imposes no ceiling on critical discussion and writing. Independent learning time is also essential for above grade level students, as it is for all students. Care must be taken, however, to ensure that when higher achieving students work independently, they do more than pace themselves through kits or workbooks. Activities should be meaningful.

In some cases high achievers were overused in helping their peers. While cooperative learning and peer tutoring benefits both stronger and weaker readers (Cohen, Kulik, & Kulik, 1982), excessive reliance on stronger students can result in students reporting that they "feel used, resentful, and frustrated by group work with students of lower ability" (Willis, 1990, p. 10). Slavin (1991) reports that students in the top 33%, 10%, and 5% of the student body of two cooperative schools outperformed a control group on standardized test scores. The cooperative programs incorporated flexible grouping within the class and therefore differentiated instruction for students of different achievement levels. Slavin attributes the success of cooperative learning with high achievers (a) to peer encouragement to learn (it benefits the group), and (b) to the fact that we learn best by describing our knowledge to others. When high achievers help their peers, they should evaluate what students already know, rethink and reorganize concepts, and demonstrate and explain ideas clearly. In doing so effectively, higher achievers extend and clarify their own thinking (Routman, 1991).

➤ **4. Limited Number of Grouping Options in Use.** In some cases, teachers lost the "flexible" in flexible grouping, becoming comfortable with using a limited number of grouping options rather than exploring different options based on curricular goals and individual needs. Teachers with self-contained classes seemed to be able to manage a variety of grouping patterns more easily than those who specialized in reading and language arts. Some of the specialized teachers felt constrained by limited morning and afternoon time blocks and their perceived responsibility to fit everything in.

One grouping option that took some time to develop was the use of centers. Although the number and uses of centers in the primary grades increased in some flexibly grouped classrooms, centers were sparse in particular in those rooms where whole-group instruction was predominant. As teachers began to see centers as a way to provide choice time for students while the teachers meet with small groups or individual children, learning centers became more evident.

➤ **5. Limited Time for Scheduling Almost-Daily Extra Help Groups.** Scheduling almost-daily extra help groups has been difficult, especially in classes with many struggling readers. As a Grade 1 teacher commented, "I'm afraid I am not meeting the needs of my lowest students. I just don't know how to find the time to help them and I don't know *exactly* how to help them." Another primary teacher commented, "I am finding that strategies like echo reading and using boxes (a phonemic awareness activity) are benefitting my low students, but I still find it hard to schedule them. Sometimes I feel they are being shortchanged." The issue of what to do with the other children is also raised frequently. Successful teachers (a) differentiate assignments to be sure no students are practicing on a frustration level, (b) use center or choice time to meet with struggling students, and (c) provide independent or cooperative authentic reading and writing activities.

➤ **6. Difficulty with Identification of Needs, and Measurement and Reporting of Progress.** Many teachers felt insecure about their knowledge of students' specific strengths and weaknesses, and felt some discomfort in not identifying specific reading levels for them. Some had not yet developed the kidwatching (Goodman, 1991) skills or acquired the knowledge of classroom assessment necessary for them to have a firm handle on their students' progress. Consequently, they were not sure how to set up needs-based groups or otherwise meet the individual needs of all their students.

Measuring and reporting progress is a concern to teachers, parents, and supervisors as we wrestle with ways to accurately assess in order to guide instructional decisions and communicate progress. In the past many teachers have evaluated student products (e.g., tests, compositions, worksheets) in relationship to a specified reading level and reading group. With flexible grouping, they are forced to evaluate and report the progress of students often in relation to their use of a common text and in relation to their use of a variety of materials. They must assess and report the strengths and weaknesses of those who can handle a common text with a lot of help, students who can handle the same text with only a little help, and students who can extend the text. Teachers are finding success as they move toward performance-based assessments like running records (Clay, 1979) and observational notes. This issue is developed more fully in Chapter 6.

In conferring with each other and with other district-level supervisors, we quickly discovered that teachers from other districts were having some of the same difficulties as they transitioned from ability grouping to a flexible-grouping model of instruction. We also learned that teachers were asking to visit each other so they could observe flexible grouping in action. In Pinellas County, in an effort to meet the need to see other teachers, a Grade 1 and Grade 3 teacher were videotaped, and the tape was distributed to all seventy-seven elementary schools.

Now that we have completed a third year, some of our concerns are gradually diminishing. Many teachers have extra help groups. Some of these are heterogeneous and others are organized by performance level. Some teachers say that they are feeling more comfortable about varying instruction for students. They want to know how to help struggling students. They are asking for more information about teaching strategies and want to attend more conferences and read more literature. Probably the most difficult task for teachers continues to be finding a balance between whole-group and small-group instruction. Some teachers continue to comment that finding a schedule that works for all students is difficult and involves a lot of planning. Yet, they remain enthusiastic about flexible grouping. As one teacher said after rattling off a list of complaints, "but you know, I wouldn't go back to the old way for the world!"

CONCLUDING REMARKS

As we promised at the beginning of this chapter, preparing for change in grouping patterns is no easy task. And it is said that the only person who likes change is a wet baby. It all seems worthwhile, however, when we hear words such as the following from a flexibly-grouped class (Paratore, 1991):

"I felt good about Myself because i never read a hole book with little help. I only read wone book before when i was 5."—FRED, Grade 4

We have just begun to learn about the impact of flexible grouping. We see a need for more research, especially classroom action research, into the needs of students of varying abilities; the attitudes of students, parents, and teachers; and flexible-grouping models that are particularly effective. We are aware, too, that as teaching practices change within flexible-grouping models, it will be more difficult to look at the impact of flexible grouping without considering the impact of such variables as changing student and teacher roles. There are still concerns and unanswered questions. Nonetheless, the evidence to date indicates that this model of instruction can and does work for teachers and students. We believe its full potential is yet to be realized.

REFERENCES

Atwell, N. (1987). *In the middle: Writing, reading, and learning with adolescents*. Portsmouth, NH: Heinemann.

Berghoff, B., & Egawa, K. (1991). No more "rocks": Grouping to give students control of their learning. *The Reading Teacher, 44*, 536–541.

Clay, M. M. (1979). *The early detection of reading difficulties*, 3rd ed. Portsmouth, NH: Heinemann.

Cohen, P. A., Kulik, J. A., & Kulik, C. C. (1982). Educational outcomes of tutoring: A meta-analysis of findings. *American Educational Research Association, 19*, 237–248.

Cunningham, P. (1991). Research directions: Multimethod, multi-level literacy instruction in first grade. *Language Arts, 68*, 578–584.

Goodman, Y. (1991). Kidwatching includes kidlistening as well. In R. S. Goodman, L. B. Bird, & Y. M. Goodman (Eds.), *Whole language catalog*, p. 208. Santa Rosa, CA: American School Publishers.

Hansen, J. (1987). *When writers read*. Portsmouth, NH: Heinemann.

Hiebert, E. H. (1987). The context of instruction and student learning: An examination of Slavin's assumptions. *Review of Educational Research, 57*, 337–340.

Hiebert, E. H. (1991). Research directions: Literacy contexts and literacy processes. *Language Arts, 68*, 134–139.

Joyce, B., & Showers, B. (1982). The coaching of teaching. *Educational Leadership, 40*(1), 4–10.

Paratore, J. (1991). *Flexible grouping: Why and how*. The Leadership Letters: Issues and Trends in Reading and Language Arts. Columbus, OH: Silver Burdett & Ginn.

Radencich, M. C. (1992). Integrated lesson plan formats: How do you fit it all in? *Florida Reading Quarterly, 29*(2), 15–17.

Radencich, M. C. (1993). Curiouser and curiouser... *The Reading Teacher, 47,* 173–175.

Richek, M. A., & Glick, L. C. (1991). Coordinating a literacy support program with classroom instruction. *The Reading Teacher, 44,* 474–479.

Routman, R. (1991). *Invitations: Changing as teachers and learners K–12.* Portsmouth, NH: Heinemann.

Slavin, R. E. (1991). Are cooperative learning and "untracking" harmful to the gifted? *Educational Leadership, 48*(6), 68–71.

Willis, S. (1990). Cooperative learning fallout. *ASCD Update, 32*(8), 6–8.

▶ 6

Connecting Assessment and Instruction in the Flexibly-Grouped Classroom

JEANNE R. PARATORE

Imagine a typical week in a classroom where flexible grouping represents the organizational plan. On one day, you might observe students previewing a book or chapter and making predictions about it. Later, you might watch students read a chapter or an article silently and compose a written response. On another day, you might see students reread a chapter or an article and discuss it in a small group with their classmates. Then, you might see them select a favorite part and reread it orally. Sometimes you will see the students working with the whole class, at other times with a small group or, at yet other times, individually. Sometimes you will observe them receiving a lot of help from a teacher or a peer; at other times, they will work alone.

As you gather observations, which should you judge important? Which of these displays of literacy should count as a legitimate assessment or as documentation of the student's literacy knowledge? How should you grade the performance if the child received help from the teacher or from a peer?

This chapter explores assessment in the flexibly-grouped classroom. It examines these questions and suggests ways teachers can use the observations they gather from daily literacy events to monitor and document literacy learning and to plan appropriate, responsive instruction. In the first section, beliefs about literacy that underlie the flexibly-grouped classroom are explored. Then, ways those beliefs are connected to assessment practices are presented, along with examples shared by teachers in elementary classrooms.

CONNECTING BELIEFS ABOUT LITERACY TO ASSESSMENT PRACTICES

Literacy instruction within the heterogeneously grouped classroom is based on an understanding that literacy knowledge is dynamic rather than static, changing on the basis of the conditions and contexts under which it is practiced. Studies suggest literacy performances may vary on the basis of several aspects related to the text itself, such as whether or not it is familiar or unfamiliar, fiction or nonfiction, high interest or low interest, or perhaps even long or short (Asher, 1980; Brown, Campione, Webber, & McGilly, 1992; Herman, 1985; Hunt, 1970; Johnston, 1992). A teacher might observe, for example, a child who loves snakes is able to read a seemingly difficult encyclopedia entry on snakes with ease, and later observe that same student struggle with a passage judged to be of similar difficulty about cornfields, a topic about which the child knows little. The apparent incongruence in these performances is consistent with what is known about the influence of background knowledge and interest on reading performance.

A similar shift in performance may occur when the nature of the instructional setting or the interactions between the student and the teacher or peers changes during a literacy event (see Roehler & Duffy, 1991, for a comprehensive review of related studies). Depending on the literacy task, the benefit of a teacher-led demonstration may boost some children toward success, collaboration with a small group of peers may enable other children to succeed, while an opportunity to practice individually and independently may be sufficient for others.

Teaching literacy within a heterogeneously grouped classroom is also based on the assumption that literacy is multiple, rather than singular, characterized not by one ability or performance but, instead, by many. In classrooms, children develop many different literacies, including oral retellings, oral readings, book discussions, personal responses to selections read, and oral or written summaries of selections. Teachers often think of these as literacy tasks, and the nature of the assigned task itself may influence students' performances (Brown, Campione, Webber & McGilly, 1992; Gardner,

1992). Virtually every student can compose some type of written response to a selection heard or read. Only some students might be able to perform a fluent oral reading of a particular text. Some may be particularly strong at composing an oral or written summary while others are able to elaborate and clarify, recalling and organizing specific details to justify their response.

The work samples of a second-grade child named Jennifer provide one example of how different factors come together to influence a student's literacy performance. In the first example (Figure 6-1), Jennifer was asked to display her understanding of a story by answering questions on a worksheet. This work sample was completed independently, after a silent reading of the selection.

Jennifer's performance was clearly limited. When viewed alone, it might suggest she is unable to read and comprehend this particular text successfully. When joined with a second performance sample, however, the picture of her literacy knowledge changes. In the second example (Figure 6-2), Jennifer was asked to reread the same selection. This time, she was given an opportunity to discuss it with the teacher and a small group of children and to take some written notes. She was then asked to compose a written summary.

This second performance provides a very different assessment of Jennifer's literacy, suggesting that under appropriate instructional conditions, she is able to read and comprehend the text successfully. The clear difference in Jennifer's literacy performance was not accomplished by changing the text to easier material, but rather by providing her more practice (a rereading), more support (a collaborative discussion and a framework for taking notes), and a more contextualized task for displaying her knowledge (a written summary rather than a list of discrete questions). In this classroom, the teacher varied the instructional conditions to provide Jennifer the most optimal conditions for developing and practicing her literate abilities. The teacher was careful to document both Jennifer's performances under conditions of substantial help and of little help, and to use each to develop an understanding of the full range of Jennifer's abilities at this point in time.

In classrooms where flexible grouping is most effective, teachers use students' routine literacy performances not only for purposes of evaluation, but also to plan instruction. As Jennifer's teacher did, they collect samples that document students' performances under different instructional conditions, on different literacy tasks, and on different types of text. They then use those samples to plan and guide both their grouping decisions and their instructional strategies. An effective and increasingly popular way to accomplish these tasks is to implement a portfolio assessment system in the classroom. In the next section, guidelines are provided for joining portfolio assessment with flexible grouping.

1. Where did Walter Dean Myers grow up?

grow up New York City.

2. How did Mr. Myers become a writer?

He was raed and He like to

3. How did Mr. Myers feel about reading and writing when he was young?

4. In what way is Mr. Myers like his father and grandfather?

5. How might this interview with Walter Dean Myers help you if you want to become a writer?

6. If an interviewer asked how you feel about reading and writing, what would you say?

FIGURE 6-1   Lee Bennett Hopkins Interviews Walter Dean Myers

Jen

Walter Dean Myers was
born in Martinsburg West Virginia
he was adoped when He was lived
in Harlem New York City He read
aloud to his mother When she
did hous work. H boghta
typereter. He Wtore a story
entered a cohtest and won the
cohtest.

FIGURE 6-2   Jennifer's Second Performance Sample

CONNECTING ASSESSMENT PRINCIPLES TO ROUTINE INSTRUCTIONAL PRACTICE

As with grouping practices, portfolio assessment is framed by the evidence that literacy is dynamic, rather than static, and multiple, rather than singular, leading to four guiding principles.

First, since literacy performances change based on the context or the setting where they occur, the setting in which the child most frequently receives instruction provides the best measure of students' schoolbased literacies. Therefore, performance samples should emerge from contexts during which daily classroom tasks and literacy events occur, rather than from periods and tasks set aside for testing and evaluation. Such contexts include events that occur before reading such as individual or paired prediction making, question asking, or selection previewing; events that occur during reading such as silent reading, partner reading, think-alouds (Davey, 1983), or note taking; and events that occur after reading such as individual retelling, journal writing, and student-led or teacher-led discussion groups.

Second, since literacy performances change across different tasks, samples should represent the full range of literate behaviors developed and practiced in classrooms, including written tasks such as summaries and descriptions of selections and books read; evidence of oral reading fluency; contributions to book discussions; and oral retellings. In addition, literacy performances should represent different types of text, including fiction and nonfiction, familiar and unfamiliar, high interest and low interest.

Third, since literacy performances change based on different instructional contexts, samples should be drawn under an array of conditions: when the student performs with substantial help from the teacher or a peer (e.g., a demonstration or a model); a moderate amount of help (e.g., guided practice from the teacher or a cooperative learning situation with a peer or a small group of peers); and no help (e.g., situations where the student performs the task individually and independently).

Fourth, since evidence suggests self-awareness leads to the ability to control and create conditions for success (Paris, Wasik, & Turner, 1991), it is critical that students be integrally involved in the assessment process, engaging in systematic and routine opportunities to reflect on their own work, assess their performances (e.g., identify artifacts that represent their best work, greatest effort, or easiest task), and describe the conditions that lead to success.

Essentially, four steps are necessary if teachers are to connect assessment to routine instructional practice: establishing benchmarks, establishing a system for collecting portfolio samples, establishing a system for reviewing and summarizing information in the portfolio, and using information in the portfolio. Each of these steps is described below.

Establishing Benchmarks

The first step to monitoring students' literacy learning is the establishment of benchmarks or abilities they are expected to achieve at the end of each grade level. These benchmarks become the template or the lens through which teachers view their students' literacy performances and plan instruction. It is useful to keep the benchmarks global enough to apply across grade levels. This permits teachers at each grade to specify the evidence they use to evaluate whether or not students are progressing toward the benchmark.

For example, in one school where I work, the teachers established the following general literacy benchmarks:

1. Students are able to establish a purpose or focus attention in preparation for reading.
2. Students are able to organize information effectively during and after reading.
3. Students are able to elaborate and clarify information to answer questions and explain and justify responses.

4. Students are able to compose a summary of information.
5. Students are able to use decoding strategies when encountering unknown words.
6. Students are able to self-monitor each of the above literacy behaviors and fix up as appropriate.
7. Students are able to use literacy "to get things done."
8. Students are able to develop an interest in and a love of reading.

Teachers then used the benchmarks to formulate questions to guide their review of each student's literacy portfolio:

1. What is the evidence that the student establishes a purpose or focuses attention in preparation for reading? (e.g., students were observed paging through a selection or chapter before reading, pausing at illustrations or making comments to a partner; students were observed making predictions with a partner; journal entries provided a record of logical prediction making; when reading content area text, students were observed previewing questions at the end of the chapter before reading or asking questions about technical vocabulary)
2. What is the evidence that the student effectively organizes information during and after reading? (e.g., effective use of story or idea maps [Armbruster & Anderson, 1982]; retellings organized sequentially or categorically)
3. What is the evidence that the student elaborates and clarifies information? (e.g., written responses, drawings, or ideas shared during book discussions that include information not explicitly stated in the text; responses that relate a text or an event to other texts read or to the student's own life; responses that relate explicitly and implicitly the details of an essential part of the story, such as the setting, problem, solution or consequence)
4. What is the evidence that the student summarizes information read? (e.g., oral or written summaries provide a clear organizational framework such as description, cause/effect, comparison/contrast, or sequence; eliminate redundancy and trivial information; use superordinate terms to incorporate subordinate ideas; begin or end with a topic sentence)*
5. What is the evidence that the student uses decoding strategies when encountering unknown words? (e.g., audiotapes, running records, and anecdotal records gathered during partner reading document students' awareness and application of decoding strategies; spellings in written samples display knowledge of appropriate sound/symbol relationships)

*These criteria are based on Ann Brown and Jeanne Day, *Macrorules for Summarizing Texts: The Development of Expertise* (Urbana, IL: Center for the Study of Reading, 1983).

6. What is the evidence that the student self-monitors and fixes up as appropriate? (e.g., students are observed: rereading or looking back at text when they are confused or unable to answer a question or participate in a discussion; seeking help from teachers and peers appropriately; initiating appropriate reading strategies, such as previewing text, taking written notes when appropriate, making a map to organize ideas; engaging in revision of written work; making logical choices in choosing representative samples of their work)

7. What is the evidence that the student uses literacy "to get things done?" (e.g., students are observed: reading and writing to accomplish everyday tasks, such as note writing as reminders to themselves or others; letter writing to communicate ideas; and reading to find information)

8. What is the evidence that the student is developing an interest in and a love of literacy? (e.g., students are observed: reading and writing to pass the time; talking about their favorite books and authors; sharing their writing with others)

Collecting Portfolio Samples

After benchmarks are formulated, the next step in implementing a portfolio system is to create a system or framework for collecting portfolio samples. The general principles outlined earlier in this chapter provide the basis for the following classroom practices:

- Collecting samples should be routine and systematic, so the portfolio represents a collection of performances over time and across contexts, rather than a single episode or event.
- Work samples to be included in the portfolio should be selected by students. Student selection not only develops ownership in the portfolio process, but it also supports the development of reflection on their own work and assessment of the conditions that led to ease or difficulty, success or failure.
- A standard entry in the portfolio should be a log of books or articles read and the students' evaluations of those selections, allowing teachers and students to develop an understanding of reading interests and the choices that students make (Figure 6-3).
- Since much literate behavior is observed rather than written, portfolio entries should represent artifacts that document observations, as well as written products. This means that in addition to students' selections of written products, teachers will also place anecdotal notes in the portfolios, documenting their observations of the ways students practice literacy and of the conditions that promote success. Anecdotal comments might address students' participation in student-led groups or pairs,

NAME _____

Month _____

What Did I Read?

Date Started	Book Title and Author	Date Finished	Easy, Hard, or Just Right?	What Do I Think?

Look at all the books you read this month. Which one did you like best? On the back of this paper tell what it is and why you liked it.

FIGURE 6-3 Book Log

students' oral reading fluency during partner readings, students' uses of literacy during recreational periods, students' strategic reading behaviors such as previewing text or illustrations, or students' uses of various fix-up strategies such as rereadings or text lookbacks.

- Teachers may organize their anecdotal comments in different ways. Some teachers develop forms such as those presented in Figures 6-4 and 6-5, and set aside a routine time to circulate and record observations of students' literacy practices. These observations are transferred into the portfolios of individual students after school or during a planning period. Instead of using a list of predetermined behaviors, some teachers keep a clipboard close by with a sheet of self-adhesive labels on which they record observations and anecdotes about literacy behaviors. These labels are later transferred into individual portfolios.

Building on the recommendations of Tierney, Carter, and Desai (1991), many teachers have students keep two types of performance sample collec-

	Listens for a Target Element	Locates Target Sound in Words	Tracks Words	Engages in Choral Reading
Marcus				
Nicholas				
Erin				
Kristen				
Mathew				
Simon				
Maria				
Christopher				
Todd				
Nicole				
Emily				

FIGURE 6-4 Assessing Beginning Reading Strategies

	Chooses Appropriate Books	Returns to the Text to Elaborate/Clarify	Uses Book Project to Synthesize Ideas	Presents Ideas to Class Clearly
Julia				
Arnoldo				
Jose				
Tany Ban				
Hiew				
Elissa				
Takara				
Christopher				
Richard				
Nicole				
Elaina				

FIGURE 6-5 Assessing Reading Workshop Strategies

tions: a working folder in which they place all artifacts of their literacy knowledge and a showcase portfolio in which they place their purposeful selections, e.g., samples of their best work, the piece they worked hardest on, the piece they are proudest of. As students shift their work samples from the working folder to the showcase portfolio, it is helpful for them to attach a label or a form describing the reason for selection and the context in which it was completed (Figure 6-6).

Reviewing and Summarizing Information in the Portfolio

Once the portfolio begins to build, the teacher must establish a way to use the information to construct a biography or a profile of the child's literacy

Date chosen: _____

Why I chose this piece:

_____

_____

_____

I did this work:

Alone _____

With a partner _____

With a small group _____

With the teacher _____

FIGURE 6-6   Portfolio Sample

knowledge and to make decisions about the student's instructional needs. In keeping with the principles outlined above, the profile should describe not only the range of performances, but also the conditions under which the various performances were achieved. Further, it should join the student's performance samples to the benchmarks or questions posed at the outset. The chart presented in Figure 6-7 provides an example of one way to join these three principles.

In this example, the benchmarks or questions provide a lens through which to view each performance sample. Multiple samples are recorded on a single form, enabling teachers and students to examine any patterns that emerge, and a fairly simple key represents the amount of scaffolding or support students needed to achieve the benchmarks. This particular marking key uses pluses, rather than minuses, to describe increased levels of instructional support. Students learn to associate knowing when to ask for help as a useful and wise learning strategy rather than a symbol of failure. Space for additional comments allows teachers to record any other notes about conditions for success. The chart may be completed by the student and the teacher in collaboration or by the teacher alone. If completed by the teacher alone, it should be shared, explained, and discussed with the student

NAME _____ GRADE _____ MONTH _____

BENCHMARKS

Work Sample	Uses Decoding/ Encoding Strategies	Sets Purpose	Organizes Information	Elaborates and Clarifies	Summarizes	Self-Monitors	Uses Literacy "to Get Things Done"	Demonstrates Interest in and Love of Literacy	Comments

√ no help   √+ some help   √++ a lot of help

COMMENTS:

FIGURE 6-7 Constructing a Literacy Profile: Aggregating Data in a Portfolio

during an individual conference. It may also be used to frame the presentation of showcase portfolio contents during parent/teacher or parent/teacher/child conferences.

Using Portfolio Samples to Plan Instruction

In a second-grade classroom where students had all read *Thomas' Snowsuit* by Robert Munsch, students were asked to take the role of Thomas in the story and compose a letter to their mothers describing what had happened to them in school that day. Prior to assigning the written response, the teacher offered the children several different literacy experiences. As a whole class, children had listened to the text first. Then some children reread it silently and discussed it in small groups. Other students met with the teacher and received some practice on key vocabulary, reread the selection with a partner, and then discussed it in a small group. As can be seen in the two examples displayed in Figures 6-8 and 6-10, the students in this classroom have a wide range of performance on this task. Peter is a student with strong literacy abilities. He worked in a student-led cooperative group and composed the written response, displayed in Figure 6-8.

When compared against the benchmarks that the teachers established for this classroom, this work sample provides evidence of clear organization with sequential details, extensive elaboration of individual events, and clarification through the use of figurative language *(in a flash, what a disaster)*. In recording this entry on the aggregation form (Figure 6-9), the teacher noted that Peter completed this task without help from the teacher or a peer. She also noted that since he was able to do this with relatively little instructional support, he would probably benefit from opportunities that would challenge him by perhaps doing an author study of several of Munsch's works, or by comparing one of Munsch's works to a book by a different author. She makes a a note to check with Peter on which of the literacy tasks might interest him most.

Another student in this classroom, Rene, speaks English as a second language and, prior to this year, had been placed in a special education classroom. He received substantial extra help from the teacher in reading this book, including several opportunities to partner read the text. Rene's written response (Figure 6-10), although limited, provides evidence that he is making progress toward some of the established benchmarks. He retold the beginning, middle, and end, suggesting that he has acquired one strategy for summarizing a story.

In recording this sample on the aggregation form (Figure 6-11), the teacher noted there were specific conditions that enabled Rene to succeed on this task: He received substantial help in the form of vocabulary practice and several rereadings. She noted he needs to continue to receive individual

Peter

Dear mom,
I did not want to go out for recess because I had to wear my snowsuit. The teacher made me wear it but I said nnnn no! I had a fight with the teacher because I did not want to wear my snowsuit. The teacher treid to stik me and the snowsuit together. But they where in a not. The next thing I no I'm in my underwear. And then the principal came in and got into the fight. And then they treid to put on my snowsuit. But when we had the fight the teacher was wearing the principal's suit the principal was wearing the teachers dress and I was lafing my head-off. I was still in my under-wear. When the principal and the teacher was arguing. one of my friends told me. And then I got on my snowsuit on and then I went out to play in a flash. The next day the principal was in Arizona. I hope the never ever hapins agen. What a dizaster.

To mom
from thomis

FIGURE 6-8   Peter's Portfolio Sample

NAME __Peter__   GRADE __2__   MONTH __March__

BENCHMARKS

Work Sample	Uses Decoding/ Encoding Strategies	Sets Purpose	Organizes Information	Elaborates and Clarifies	Summarizes	Self-Monitors	Uses Literacy "to Get Things Done"	Demonstrates Interest in and Love of Literacy	Comments
Thomas' snowsuit (Letter)	✓ (Great Spelling!)		✓ (Well-sequenced)	✓ (Used figurative lang.)					give opportunity to read and compare other Munsch books

✓ no help   ✓+ some help   ✓++ a lot of help

COMMENTS:

FIGURE 6-9 Constructing a Literacy Profile: Aggregating Data in a Portfolio (Peter)

Rene

Dear mom,
the teacher and the principal I had a
fight a School.
The teacher ak me butan my snowsuit.
I said. "NNNN NNoo
The teacher and me had a fight.
form thomgs.

FIGURE 6-10 Rene's Portfolio Sample

129

NAME **Rene**   GRADE **2**   MONTH **March**

Work Sample	Uses Decoding/ Encoding Strategies	Sets Purpose	Organizes Information	Elaborates and Clarifies	Summarizes	Self-Monitors	Uses Literacy "to Get Things Done"	Demonstrates Interest in and Love of Literacy	Comments
Thomas' Snowsuit (Letter)			✓++ Retold 1st, next, last	✓++ Retold beg, mid, end					Read this story 4x before writing

no help   + some help   ++ a lot of help

COMMENTS:

FIGURE 6-11 Constructing a Literacy Profile: Aggregating Data in a Portfolio (Rene)

help in decoding strategies and would benefit from small-group instruction reading easier books. She also noted that she needs to obtain a running record (Clay, 1979) of his word-identification strategies when reading easier text, to judge and plan small-group or individual instruction to meet Rene's specific decoding needs.

In examining this teacher's use of portfolio samples to judge performance and plan instruction, there are several practices that stand out. First, since in this example the teacher had used a common reading as the instructional text, it was important that she provide a criterion task accessible to everyone regardless of his or her literacy proficiency. By choosing written response as the criterion task, both Peter and Rene were able to display their understanding. As the samples reveal, the types of written response varied dramatically, yet each student was able to share in the experience. Second, when judging the criterion tasks, the teacher used a template or a lens that enabled her to observe and record each student's areas of strength and the conditions under which they were performed. Therefore, the same task allowed her to establish Peter's proficiency with elaboration and clarification and Rene's proficiency with organization and summarization. Finally, she used the portfolio system to note the ways the student might be supported and challenged, informing the grouping decisions that must be made in a classroom characterized by changing and dynamic groups. Although this example captures the review of only a single performance sample, it is assumed this sample will be joined by others and, as the teacher proceeds through the portfolio, the students' literacy profiles will continue to expand.

CONCLUDING REMARKS

The purpose of classroom assessment should be to describe the conditions under which children are able to accomplish the goals and objectives set forth at each grade level, so that teachers can create those conditions in their classrooms. The system of assessment described here is designed specifically to provide teachers a way to systematically collect information about how students perform routine instructional tasks, and to help them to plan instruction and optimize students' learning by supporting the development of flexible small groups to meet individual needs. The system is easy in that it requires no special materials, no specialized assessment strategies or tasks, and no additional instructional time. Assessment is entirely situated within the context of ongoing instruction. Further, it is based on a belief that any literacy event important enough to occur within the instructional setting is worthy of becoming the basis for assessment. It is challenging, however, in that collecting the information is only the first step. To make sense of the information, teachers will need to take time to reflect on the collection, plan, and respond to students' instructional needs. When they do so, the benefits are far-reaching. Consider, for example, the comments of Irene, the Chapter 1 teacher of second-grader Jennifer whose work was presented earlier in this chapter:

I felt like the voice-over in a recent pre-core evaluation team meeting about Jennifer. Repeating second grade this year, she was not meeting up to her classroom teacher's expectations. The first meeting was filled with "She can't . . . , She can't . . . ," and "This is her second time in second grade so she should . . ." I knew there were tasks she didn't do well or just didn't do in class, and, maybe a year ago, I would have echoed her teacher's sentiment. But that day I sat armed with evidence that deserved notice, evidence that challenged some of the "can't do." So when many at the meeting were hearing and seeing what she couldn't do, I was the voice-over that said, "Yes, but look at what she is doing now that she wasn't doing last year. Look at what she's written. Look at how she acts. Look at her positive attitude. She's learning."

Keeping a portfolio and following the same child for two years armed me with enough ammunition to make that voice-over loud enough to be heard. Would my script have been the same a year ago? I doubt it. Would Jennifer still be in a regular second-grade classroom? I tend to doubt that too.

For me, keeping the portfolio has been a questioning experience. I didn't really know what I had until I periodically sat down at the dining room table and reflected on its contents. For Jennifer, it's been a voice that said, "It might take me a while, and I'll probably need your help, but look at me. I CAN do it!"

REFERENCES

Armbruster, B. B., & Anderson, T. H. (1982). *Idea mapping: The technique and its use in the classroom* (Reading Education Report No. 36). Urbana: University of Illinois, Center for the Study of Reading.

Asher, S. (1980). Topic interest and children's reading comprehension. In R. J. Spiro, B. C. Bruce, & W. F. Breser (Eds.), *Theoretical issues in reading comprehension* (pp. 525–534). Hillsdale, NJ: Erlbaum.

Brown, A. L., Campione, J. C., Webber, L. S., & McGilly, K. (1992). Interactive learning environments: A new look at assessment and instruction. In B. R. Gifford & M. C. O'Connor (Eds.), *Changing assessments: Alternative views of aptitude, achievement, and instruction* (pp. 121–212). Boston: Kluwer.

Brown, A. L., & Day, J. (1983). *Macrorules for summarizing text: The development of expertise*. Urbana, IL: Center for the Study of Reading.

Clay, M. (1979). *The early detection of reading difficulties* (3rd ed.). Portsmouth, NH: Heinemann.

Davey, B. (1983). Think-aloud—Modeling the cognitive processes of reading comprehension. *Journal of Reading, 27*, 444–447.

Gardner, H. (1992). Assessment in context: The alternative to standardized testing. In B. R. Gifford & M. C. O'Connor (Eds.), *Changing assessments: Alternative views of aptitude, achievement, and instruction* (pp. 77–120). Boston: Kluwer.

Herman, P. A. (1985). The effect of repeated readings on reading rate, speech pauses, and word recognition accuracy. *Reading Research Quarterly, 20*, 553–565.

Hunt, L. (1970). The effect of self-selection, interest, and motivation upon independent, instructional, and frustrational levels. *The Reading Teacher, 24*, 146–151.

Johnston, P. H. (1992). *Constructive evaluation of literacy activity.* NY: Longman.

Paris, S. G., Wasik, B. A., & Turner, J. C. (1991). The development of strategic readers. In R. Barr, M. L. Kamil, P. B. Mosenthal, & P. D. Pearson (Eds.), *Handbook of reading research* (Vol. II, pp. 609–640). NY: Longman.

Roehler, L. R., & Duffy, G. G. (1991). Teachers' instructional actions. In R. Barr, M. L. Kamil, P. B. Mosenthal, & P. D. Pearson (Eds.), *Handbook of reading research* (Vol. II, pp. 861–884). NY: Longman.

Tierney, R. J., Carter, M. A., & Desai, L. (1991). *Portfolio assessment in the reading-writing classroom.* Norwood, MA: Christopher-Gordon.

CHILDREN'S BOOKS

Munsch, R. (1985). *Thomas' snowsuit.* Art by M. Martchenko. Toronto, Canada: Annick.

▶ 7

At-Risk Children Can Learn to Read and Write

PATRICIA M. CUNNINGHAM

Each year, six million children begin kindergarten in our public schools. Many of these children can be immediately identified as at-risk—the currently popular descriptor for those children who will not learn to read and write well enough to achieve a basic level of literacy and a high school diploma. The number of children at risk varies from community to community and from state to state. Nationwide, National Assessment for Educational Progress (NAEP) results suggest more than one-third of all nine-year-olds cannot read at the basic level. For African-Americans, 61% fail to achieve this basic level (Mullis & Jenkins, 1990).

These statistics—horrifying as they are—have held fairly constant despite decades of expensive attempts to "fix" the problem. Federal fix-ups have generally included a variety of pull-out remediation programs spawning huge bureaucracies that have not succeeded in eliminating the risk for very many children.

State and local fix-ups often consisted of passing regulations prohibiting children being promoted unless they obtained certain test scores; as a result huge numbers of children were retained. Shepard and Smith (1990) reviewed decades of research on retention. They estimate that by 1990, half of all ninth graders had been retained at least one time. Their data show retained children perform more poorly when they go to the next grade than they would have if they had been promoted without repeating, and that almost any alternative is more effective than retention. Their data also suggest that transition classes, when they result in all children spending another year in the primary grades, have the same ill effects as retention.

Within individual schools or classrooms, in addition to federally provided remediation and state or locally mandated retention, teachers usually try to meet the needs of at-risk children by putting them in a bottom reading group and pacing instruction more slowly. The data on bottom groups do not hold out much hope that this solution will ultimately solve the problem. Children who are placed in the bottom group in first grade generally remain there throughout their elementary school career and almost never learn to read and write up to grade level standards (Allington, 1983, 1991).

By 1987, when the kindergartners who should graduate in the year 2000 entered school, most educators realized the usual diet of pull-out remediation, retention, and bottom-group placement was not going to provide the nourishment needed to transform those children who entered school at-risk into strong, healthy readers. Efforts were undertaken by a variety of schools, groups, and individuals to figure out a new, improved, and more balanced diet! In the remainder of this chapter, I will describe efforts at the school, classroom, and special teacher/remediation level that demonstrate we can transform most at-risk children into capable, successful readers and writers. I will give a description of each effort and then suggest the elements all these successful efforts have in common. (The space limitations of a chapter dictate that all descriptions be brief and simplistic. They will not begin to do justice to the intricacies that make each program work. I apologize to the program developers/implementers and recommend that readers of this chapter go to the original sources to get a true flavor of the programs, none of which are quick fixes.) Note that any program is only as good as its implementation. Moreover, those who wish to replicate successful programs must walk the fine line between adherence to carefully thought-out procedures and adaptation to local needs.

SCHOOLWIDE MODELS

Accelerated Schools

The accelerated schools model was developed by Henry Levin and colleagues at Stanford University and has been implemented in a variety of schools with high proportions of at-risk children (Knight & Stallings, 1994; Levin, 1991). The model involves the collaboration of university and school personnel in a restructuring of the entire school. Individual schools make decisions about what their priorities are and set the day-to-day implementation of goals, but all accelerated schools have the following common, broad goals: (1) the creation of a learning environment characterized by high expectations; (2) the elimination of the achievement gap for at-risk children by the end of elementary school; (3) the daily implementation of a fast-paced curriculum focusing on student engagement; and (4) involvement and empowerment of teachers and parents.

Teachers in accelerated schools are involved in inservice before implementation. They meet together on a regular basis to monitor their own progress and to make decisions on how their school can progress toward the realization of the goals. Parent education and involvement projects are implemented, and parents are included in decision-making teams. All participants in accelerated schools are asked to envision the education they would desire for their own children and then to work toward finding ways to provide that same level of excellence for all the children in their school.

Accelerated schools move away from tracking and ability grouping and use a variety of cooperative groups and student tutor/partnership arrangements. Language development is seen as a real goal in every curriculum area and curriculum is integrated around themes as much as possible. These schools optimize discovery learning, hands-on and real-world experiences, and the reading and writing of authentic texts whenever possible. Efforts are made to provide opportunities for all children to engage in the arts and to become a part of extracurricular activities. All school personnel feel responsible for helping the children develop social and critical thinking skills.

Accelerated schools do not claim instant results. Teachers and administrators acknowledge that it takes several years for a school to become the accelerated school its staff and community envision. Children who come to school at-risk will not all be on grade level the first year. Teachers do, however, have high expectations (supported by their initial data) that given a long-term schoolwide effort toward clearly defined goals, school for at-risk children can look like the schools we want for our own children. Almost all at-risk children can leave elementary school with solid on-grade level reading, writing, and thinking skills.

Success for All

The Success for All program was developed by Robert Slavin and colleagues at the Center for Research on Effective Schooling for Disadvantaged Students at Johns Hopkins University (Slavin, Madden, Karweit, Livermon & Dolan, 1990; Slavin, Madden, Karweit, Dolan & Wasik, 1994). Originally implemented in one inner-city school in Baltimore, the model is currently in use in more than fifty schools in fifteen states. Success for All takes seriously Edmonds's (1981) assertion that we know enough to teach our at-risk children and that what we must now do is get it done! Success for All takes its name very seriously. Every child is expected to be a capable on-grade level reader by the end of third grade. To accomplish this goal, Success for All is a multifaceted program.

Based on the belief that "an ounce of prevention is worth a pound of cure," Success for All includes both preschool and kindergarten experiences that emphasize the development and use of language. Once children enter first grade, the literacy program is intensive, varied, and closely monitored. Based on a quarterly informal reading inventory and other assessment procedures, children are grouped for reading—across grade levels—into classes that have only one reading level to teach. Reading tutors (certified teachers) become teachers for the 90-minute reading block, thus reducing the pupil-teacher ratio for this block to fifteen to one. During the 90-minute reading block, children are engaged in three activities. Each day begins with a listening comprehension lesson designed to develop language and comprehension skills. Next, the children participate in a shared story reading in which the teacher reads complex text (written in small type) and the children read simple text (written in large type). The text read by the children contains known words and words they can decode based on the letter-sound relationships learned.

Each reading block also includes decoding instruction. Children learn the letter-sound correspondences they can then apply to words they read as part of the shared story lesson. (The shared stories were written specifically for Success for All by educators at Johns Hopkins University.)

Once children achieve a first-reader instructional level in reading, their reading instruction is carried out using the Cooperative Integrated Reading and Composition (CIRC) model (Stevens, Madden, Slavin & Farnish, 1987). Children are assigned to five-member heterogeneous learning teams that complete a variety of reading activities.

In addition to their 90 minutes of reading instructional time each day, all children are involved in a daily writing/language arts activity. This writing instruction follows a writing process format. Children write first drafts and then take pieces through the revising/editing/publishing process. Children are taught mechanics within the context of skills they need for revising and editing, and they work with partners and small groups to polish their writing.

The 90-minute reading/language period and a daily process writing period are the heart of Success for All, but there are other critical components. Children's progress is assessed four times a year, and students who need assistance are provided with daily tutoring. A family support team in each school reaches out to families who need assistance in providing adequate sleep, nutrition, health care, and other needs. Each school has a full-time program facilitator, whose sole job is to work with teachers, tutors, administrators, etc., to ensure that the program is implemented as fully as possible.

Initial results for the Success for All schools are encouraging. Many more children are achieving grade level reading and writing skills. Special education referrals and placements have decreased dramatically, and retention has been reduced to nearly zero. Slavin and colleagues sum up their success and hopes for the future:

> The findings of research on Success for All and related prevention and early intervention programs make it impossible to continue to say that the problems of education in the inner city cannot be solved. The Success for All schools, which include some of the most disadvantaged schools in such cities as Baltimore, Philadelphia, Memphis, and Montgomery, Alabama, do not have unusual staffs or principals. If they can achieve success with the great majority of at-risk children, so can most schools serving similar children. It takes money, but increasingly the money is already in place as Chapter 1 funds increase for high-poverty schools, or can be found from other sources. What is most needed is leadership, a commitment at every level of the political process to see that we stop discarding so many students at the start of their school careers. (Slavin et al., 1994)

CLASSROOM MODELS

Early Intervention in Reading

The Early Intervention in Reading (EIR) program was developed by Barbara Taylor and colleagues (Taylor, Short, Shearer, & Frye, 1994). In this model, first-grade classroom teachers provide an additional 20 minutes of instruction daily to a small group (six or seven children) who are the lowest students in the class. The program has been implemented in several classrooms in Minnesota, including classrooms with a strong whole language emphasis, classrooms using systematic phonics approaches, and classrooms using a basal reader approach.

The materials for the program include actual books and story retellings. In the beginning, most instruction takes place with story retellings. The actual book is read to the class, then a short (40–60 words) retelling written on a chart is used for instruction. The length of the selections read is gradually increased as the year goes on. By the end of the year, children are reading actual books 120–160 words long. Three days are spent on each story, with specific activities outlined for each day.

On Day 1, the teacher reads the actual book to the whole class, including the children who will later be involved with the EIR activities. After the whole-class reading, the teacher reads the book (or the retelling) with the EIR group. As the teacher and small group read the story or retelling, the teacher stops at approximately five easily decodable words (short vowel words in the beginning) and models for the children how to sound and blend these words. In addition to letter-sound blending, the teacher models using context clues (What word would make sense here?). To develop their phonemic awareness, the teacher selects three words per story for the children to write in boxes (sh u t).

On Day 2, the children read and reread the story or story retelling on the chart and are reminded how to use context and sounding and blending strategies to decode unfamiliar words. They then receive their own booklet of the story, which they read and illustrate. The last page of their booklet is left blank and is used for guided writing. The children agree on one sentence to write about the story and they each write this on the last page of their own booklet. As they write, the teacher guides them to listen for the sounds in the words they can hear and tells them the spellings they are not yet able to figure out on their own. Each child then individually reads his or her story to an aide, volunteer, or older student.

Activities begun on Day 2 are completed on Day 3. Children reread their booklets individually to the teacher and finish illustrating them. After the third day, the teacher, aide, or volunteer takes a running record for each child, looking for at least 94% accuracy.

During the last quarter of the year, the children are reading real books— not retellings. At this time, the teacher stops meeting with the group and no longer does the initial story reading. Rather, she meets with pairs of students across a 3-day period and helps them independently read stories that have not been read to them first. The teacher coaches them on how to use the decoding strategies they have been taught. After a first reading with the teacher, children reread their stories with aides, volunteers, or older students.

Results of the EIR program in three different first-grade instructional approaches—whole language, systematic phonics, and basals—indicate the children involved are much more successful in learning to read than similar children without the program. Many of the children achieve grade level reading abilities by the end of the year and even those who don't quite make it to grade level develop some fluent, preprimer level reading abilities. Taylor et al. (1994) conclude:

> The program is relatively inexpensive and has been viewed favorably by classroom teachers who have provided the intervention. More importantly, the program has helped many low achieving emergent readers get off to a better start in reading in first grade than would have been the case without their participation in the program. What we find particularly exciting about the Early Intervention in Reading model is that classroom teachers are making

an important difference in the end-of-first-grade reading attainment of many of their lowest emergent readers. These teachers have made a commitment to provide 20 minutes of daily, quality supplemental reading instruction to their lowest readers, and this effort has been worthwhile.

Multimethod, Multilevel Instruction

Multimethod, Multilevel Instruction (Cunningham & Allington, 1994; Hall, Prevette, & Cunningham, 1994) is a reorganization of the classroom instructional time so that four major approaches to beginning reading are given equal time and importance. The 120 minutes normally devoted to reading/ language arts in primary classrooms is divided fairly equally among guided reading, self-selected reading, writing, and working with words. The children are not placed in groups by ability. Rather, the program meets the needs of a wide range of individual differences by providing four different methods through which children can learn, and by varying the difficulty of the materials/activities. Each block of instruction becomes as multilevel as possible.

During the Guided Reading block, all children are included in instruction centered around a particular reading selection. This selection may come from a basal reader, a Big Book, or a trade book (when multiple copies are available). Most guided reading instruction begins with a whole-class format, then moves into a partner format for reading, then back to a whole-class format for discussion and reaction. Children are not ability-grouped for this instruction but the teacher meets the needs of the below level readers by including some easy reading selections each week. When a hard selection is being read, the teacher makes sure weaker readers are partnered up with "helpful" friends. On some days, the teacher reads with a small group which may include some of the weaker readers. The major purposes of the Guided Reading block is to teach important comprehension skills/ strategies, develop word knowledge and vocabulary, develop children's listening and speaking skills, and expose children to a wide variety of literature and genres.

During the Self-Selected Reading block, children choose what they want to read from a wide variety of books and other reading materials. Children read trade books (including Big Books), books they have published, and even (occasionally) a favorite story from basal readers. For each science or social studies topic studied, the teacher gathers a variety of informational books that are popular choices during self-selected reading. Children read by themselves or with a friend. While the children read, the teacher calls individual children and makes anecdotal records on what they have chosen to read and their reading strategies. Time is provided for some children to share what they are reading at the end of this Self-Selected Reading block. In addition, the teacher often reads to the children at the beginning or end of the block.

The Writing block follows a writing process format. It begins each day with an 8–10 minute mini-lesson during which the teacher models writing. The teacher writes a short piece on an overhead transparency. As he or she writes, the teacher thinks aloud about what is written and how it is written. Writing conventions and invented spelling are modeled daily. Next, the children write on a topic they choose themselves. When the children have several pieces written, they select one to publish. Peers and the teacher help them to edit and revise the chosen piece, which they then make into a book. The daily Writing Block ends with some time in which children share what they have published or a piece-in-progress in an author's chair format.

During the Working with Words block, children develop a store of high frequency words they can automatically read and spell, and learn how to use spelling patterns to decode and spell unknown words. Two major activities take place during the daily Working with Words block—Word Wall and Making Words (Cunningham, 1991; Cunningham & Cunningham, 1992). The Word Wall is a bulletin board to which the teacher adds approximately five words each week. These are common words that have been introduced during the Guided Reading block or words the children use frequently in their daily writing. The words are written on colored pieces of paper attached to the wall so that they appear in alphabetical order (by first letter only). Five new words are added each week and children practice learning to read and spell these words through a daily chanting, clapping, writing activity.

Making Words is an every-pupil response, letter manipulative activity. The children are given a limited number of letters and manipulate these letters to make words. The teacher calls out the word to be made, children make the words with individual letters at their desks, and one child makes the word with large letters in a pocket chart. In each 15-minute making-words activity, the children make small words at the beginning of the lesson and big words at the end. After using the letters to make words, the teacher leads the children in sorting the words according to a variety of semantic and letter-sound relationships and patterns.

Multimethod, Multilevel Instruction has been used in many different primary classrooms and has a different flavor in each room depending upon the teaching style of the teacher and the needs of different classes of children. What is constant and evident across the classrooms is the belief that individual differences—both in ability and in the way children most comfortably learn—are real. Children do not all learn in the same way. Multimethod, Multilevel classrooms provide four different but complimentary routes to the goal of reading and writing success. Data from these classrooms indicate that many children who entered school at-risk are reading and writing at grade level at the end of first or second grade. Even children who do not achieve that grade level standard achieve fluent reading and writing abilities at easier levels.

SPECIAL TEACHER REMEDIATION MODELS

Facilitating Reading for Optimum Growth (FROG)

FROG, Facilitating Reading for Optimum Growth (Hall, Prevette, & Cunningham, 1994) was designed to provide daily small-group instruction to children in a Chapter 1-designated school. This school implemented the four-block Multimethod, Multilevel Instruction model described in the previous section but because almost all the children in the school could be considered at-risk for reading failure, they chose to support the four blocks with an in-class small-group component. The role of existing personnel in the school was redefined to provide the number of teachers necessary to implement the program. Chapter 1 and other special teachers were organized into FROG teams and converged upon each classroom for 45 minutes each day. The students in each class were divided into small heterogeneous groups including one strong student, two or three average students, and one weak student. These groups received daily intensive instruction with one of the FROG teachers or the classroom teacher. Each FROG session included four activities 10–12 minutes in length.

All children participated in self-selected reading as part of their classroom instruction. The FROG time began with a literary discussion based on these self-selected books. This discussion focused on a particular literary element, such as author, character, plot, setting, mood, style, theme, or illustration. Children read or discussed parts of their own book related to the literary element.

The second activity of FROG, shared reading using predictable Big Books, strengthened and supported the students' reading in the Guided Reading block. Students were taught to use a variety of reading strategies including semantic, syntactic, and graphophonic cues. Punctuation, vocabulary, predictions—all teachable elements found in a particular book—became a part of the instruction as the teacher led the students to read a predictable Big Book.

The third activity included in each FROG session was the Making Words part of the Working with Words block. Children were given letters and instruction on how to manipulate those letters to make a variety of words. The emphasis focused on learning that words are made up of predictable letter patterns.

The final activity of FROG supported the classroom Writing block. During classroom instruction, all children wrote on self-selected topics. During the FROG time, the predictable Big Book provided a model for teacher-directed writing instruction, allowing the children to make the reading/writing connection. There was a prewriting activity, followed by writing, revision, editing, and sharing.

When the 45-minute FROG time ended, the FROG teachers leapt to another classroom and the classroom teacher continued instruction with the whole class in the four blocks. Reorganizing the special teachers into FROG teams provided the small-group support needed by many of the children in this high-risk school to assure their success in the four blocks.

Data from the children who completed two years of Multimethod, Multilevel Instruction along with 45 minutes of FROG small-group instruction indicate that 73% of these children read at or above grade level at the end of second grade and that even children who had not yet attained that grade level standard had measurable, fluent reading abilities in easier materials.

Reading Recovery

Reading Recovery is a one-to-one tutoring model developed by Marie Clay in New Zealand in the 1970s and brought to the United States through the Ohio State University Reading Recovery program in the mid 1980s (Clay, 1991; DeFord, Lyons, & Pinnell, 1991). Reading Recovery is designed to accelerate the literacy development of at-risk first graders by identifying the bottom 20% of the children and then providing them with an intensive daily 30-minute tutorial. Reading Recovery teachers-in-training take a yearlong graduate course in which they tutor children under the supervision of a teacher leader and attend weekly classes where they sharpen teaching skills through demonstrations and discussions of theory and practice.

Children who are placed into the Reading Recovery program are provided with daily instruction of the highest quality. Teachers determine what the child knows and what level of books the child can begin reading through an initial observation and interaction with book time called "Roaming the Known." At the end of this time, children are placed in carefully levelled books that permit the child to experience daily reading with a high level of success and fluency. Children are moved to higher levels as the teacher observes development of their self-extending systems.

There is no one model for a Reading Recovery lesson. Reading Recovery teachers spend a year of intense study and thought learning how to observe children and determine what kind of help/support to provide to any child at any point in literacy development. Most lessons do, however, contain five key components. To give you a feel for the lesson, I will summarize the lesson included in a recent *Reading Teacher* article (Pinnell, Fried, & Estice, 1990).

1. **Rereading of Familiar Stories.** Each day, the lesson begins with the child selecting favorite books the child chooses to reread. This rereading provides opportunities for fast, fluent reading. The rereading is not without challenges, however, and children have the opportunity to do some reading work—i.e., problem solving. Teachers observe how the child accomplishes this problem-solving while reading and comment when appropriate. "That's right. What you read first didn't make sense. I like the way you fixed that up yourself. Going back really helped you." (p. 284)

2. **Taking a Running Record of Text Reading.** After rereading some favorite books, the child reads the book introduced the previous day. The child is not expected to read the text perfectly. Teachers use the guideline of 90–95% accuracy to determine that text is in the appropriate range. While the child reads, the teacher watches for and records reading behaviors—i.e., substitutions, self-corrections, omissions, and insertions. After the lesson, the teacher analyzes this running record and determines how well the child is using meaning, syntax, and visual information. This daily analysis of actual reading behavior is the basis for teacher decision making about what book to introduce next and how to direct the child's attention during the next lesson. Once the child has read the text, the teacher often takes the opportunity to make one or two teaching points. "You were working hard on this page. You said, 'Cats hoot.' That word does start like 'hoot.' Does 'Cats hoot' make sense? Try it again and think what the cats and kittens are doing in this story." (p. 285)

3. **Working with Letters.** This component is included when the child is just beginning to learn about letters and print. Children work with magnetic letters or at the chalkboard to write familiar words and work on letters. This component can also happen during the writing segment which follows.

4. **Composing a Brief Message.** Each day, the child composes a brief message—usually one or two sentences. Sometimes, these sentences are extended over several days and become stories. The writing is done in a writing book opened both to a practice

page and a writing page. The child writes the words, sometimes practicing them on the practice page first. Once the child completes the writing, the teacher copies it on a sentence strip. She cuts the sentence(s) into words and the child reconstructs the message and rereads the sentence(s). "The writing component . . . is different for every child. The variability depends on the teacher's split-second decisions related to (a) what the child already knows; (b) the child's responses during the lesson; and (c) the opportunities in the text composed by the child." (p. 287)

5. **Reading a New Book.** Every lesson ends with the introduction of a new book. The teacher plans a book introduction to build on some of the specific concepts and language structures used in it. The teacher and child look at the book together and talk about the pictures in the whole book. The child then reads the book with assistance from the teacher as needed. The new book introduced today will be the book on which the running record is taken in the next lesson.

This lesson description does not begin to do justice to the intricacy and complexity of the Reading Recovery model. If "the proof of the pudding is in the eating," then we need only look at the remarkable success experienced by the Reading Recovery program and the children it recovers. Working with children in the bottom 20% of their class, Reading Recovery achieves average grade level reading ability for over 80% of the children, nationwide. Once children achieve this level (usually in sixteen weeks or less), they are discontinued from Reading Recovery. Follow-up studies indicate the vast majority of successfully discontinued children continue to meet grade level standards without additional remedial support. Districts that have implemented Reading Recovery report dramatic drops in both retention and learning disability (LD) referrals. Reading Recovery is the most successful pull-out support program ever implemented, and it is no surprise that school systems throughout the world are now finding the money to train teachers and get a Reading Recovery program in place.

Restructured Chapter 1

Not all districts have the resources or the will to implement Reading Recovery, however. Freddy Hiebert and her colleagues in Colorado (Hiebert, Colt, Catto, & Gury, 1992) developed a successful program involving special teachers with at-risk first graders. The schools in which they worked carried out whole language instruction in the classrooms. Each classroom had twenty to twenty-two children, 30% of whom received pull-out instruction through Chapter 1. The Chapter 1 program was restructured in a number of ways.

The first restructuring involved the number of first graders Chapter 1 teachers worked with at a time. Before restructuring, the Chapter 1 teacher had worked with a group of six first graders. An aide had assisted as needed. The restructured program divided the children into two groups. The three lower readiness first graders worked with the aide for the first half of the year while the more able Chapter 1 first graders had instruction with the Chapter 1 teacher. Halfway through the year, the teacher and aide switched groups. Thus, each Chapter 1 child received one-half-year's instruction with the Chapter 1 teacher in a small group of three children.

Instruction during the 30-minute period with the Chapter 1 teacher included three activities. Each session included the repeated reading of predictable books. The books contained word patterns. After reading the books, the children wrote key words from the book along with rhyming words.

For example, following several readings of the book This Is the Cake That Mack Ate, *the teacher would ask children to find the word "cake" in the book. Children would then write the word "cake" on the acetate slate, followed by other words with the same pattern like "make," "take," "bake." Following writing, children were asked to read what they had written. (Hiebert et al., pp. 555–556).*

Writing about topics of their own choice was the third activity that took place regularly during the 30-minute teaching sessions.

During the time the children worked with the aides, similar activities took place. Teachers helped aides select books and decide on word patterns to be taught. Children took home books to read with their parents. When they had read ten books, they were given a book for their home library.

Results of the Chapter 1 restructuring demonstrated clear gains for the children. More than three-quarters could read at the primer level and half could read a grade level first-reader passage on an Informal Reading Inventory (IRI) administered at the end of the year.

CONCLUDING REMARKS:
THE REALITY OF LITERACY FOR AT-RISK CHILDREN

Writing this chapter has reaffirmed my belief that we can teach almost every child to read and write with fluency and confidence. Rereading and pondering the accounts of the varied efforts of a variety of determined educators has made me even more determined to redouble my own efforts to see that children are not written off because they don't bring with them the literate backgrounds we would like all our children to enjoy. The efforts described have many differences. Some involve teachers and parents in the decision-making process more than others. Who takes responsibility for assuring the literacy of the children also varies. Although these differences are real, the similarities are more striking. All models described here include the reading of real books and the writing of real texts as critical components that receive most of the instructional time and effort. All models seek to assure that children spend some of their time reading and rereading texts in which they can identify most of the words and thus have a high level of accuracy in their reading. All models also include some direct attention to the sound-symbol system and work to see that children are applying the patterns they are learning to their actual reading and writing.

The models described here demonstrate that we know enough and, in most cases, have enough resources—time, money, and people—to make a high level of literacy a reality for all our children. The models are not mutually exclusive. Schoolwide, classroom, and special teacher efforts can be combined in different ways—like dishes at a Chinese restaurant—to suit the needs, tastes, and budgets of various education consumers. Another six million kindergartners have just entered kindergarten. We can teach them all to read and write! Let's just do it!

REFERENCES

Allington, R. L. (1983). The reading instruction provided readers of differing reading ability. *Elementary School Journal, 83,* 549–559.

Allington, R. L. (1991). Effective literacy instruction for at-risk children. In M. Knapp & P. Shields (Eds.), *Better schooling for the children of poverty: Alternatives to conventional wisdom* (pp. 9–30). Berkeley, CA: McCutchan.

Clay, M. M. (1991). *Becoming literate: The construction of inner control.* Portsmouth, NH: Heinemann.

Cunningham, P. M. (1991). *Phonics they use: Words for reading and writing.* New York: HarperCollins.

Cunningham, P. M., & Allington, R. L. (1994). *Classrooms that work: They can all read and write.* New York: HarperCollins.

Cunningham, P. M., & Cunningham, J. W. (1992). Making words: Enhancing the invented spelling-decoding connection. *The Reading Teacher, 46,* 106–107.

DeFord, D. E., Lyons, C. A., & Pinnell, G. S. (1991). *Bridges to literacy: Learning from reading recovery.* Portsmouth, NH: Heinemann.

Edmonds, R. R. (1981). Making public schools effective. *Social Policy, 12,* 56–60.

Hall, D., Prevette, C., & Cunningham, P. (1994). Eliminating ability grouping and failure in the primary grades. In R. L. Allington & S. A. Walmsley (Eds.), *No* quick fix: Rethinking literacy programs in America's elementary schools. New York: Teachers' College Press.

Hiebert, E. H., Colt, J. M., Catto, S. L., & Gury, E. C. (1992). Reading and writing of first-grade students in a restructured Chapter 1 program. *American Educational Research Journal, 29,* 545–572.

Knight, S. L., & Stallings, J. A. (1994). A case study of the implementation of the accelerated school model in an urban elementary school. In R. L. Allington & S. A. Walmsley (Eds.), *No quick fix: Rethinking literacy programs in America's elementary schools* (pp. 223–237). New York: Teachers' College Press.

Levin, H. M. (1991). Accelerating the progress of at-risk students. In A. C. Huston (Ed.), *Children in poverty.* London: Cambridge University Press.

Mullis, I.V.S., & Jenkins, L. B. (1990). *The reading report card. 1971–88.* Washington, DC: U.S. Department of Education.

Pinnell, G. S., Fried, M. D., & Estice, R. M. (1990). Reading Recovery: Learning how to make a difference. *The Reading Teacher, 43,* 282–295.

Shepard, L. A., & Smith, M. L. (1990, May). Synthesis of research on grade retention. *Educational Leadership, 47,* 84–88.

Slavin, R. E., Madden, N. A., Karweit, N. L., Dolan, L. J., & Wasik, B. A. (1994). Success for All. In E. H. Hiebert (Ed.), *Getting reading right from the start: Effective early literacy intervention.* Boston: Allyn and Bacon.

Slavin, R. E., Madden, N. A., Karweit, N. L., Liverman, B. J., & Dolan, L. (1990). Success for All: First-year outcomes of a comprehensive plan for reforming urban education. *American Educational Research Journal, 27,* 255–278.

Stevens, R. J., Madden, N. A., Slavin, R. E., & Farnish, A. M. (1987). Cooperative integrated reading and composition: Two field experiments. *Reading Research Quarterly, 22,* 433–454.

Taylor, B., Short, R., Shearer, B., & Frye, B. (1994). Teachers' commitment to early reading intervention in first grade classrooms. In R. L. Allington & S. A. Walmsley (Eds.), *No quick fix: Rethinking literacy programs in America's elementary schools* (pp. 148–163). New York: Teachers' College Press.

CHILDREN'S BOOKS

Robert, R. (1987). *The cake that Mack ate.*

Multiple Literacy Contexts in Classrooms: Frameworks, Functions, and Forecasts

ELFRIEDA H. HIEBERT

Configurations of students in classrooms—whether these are small groups of students talking about a passage, individuals writing responses to a drama, or teacher-led lessons about story elements—differ from one another in ways much more substantive than the number of students involved or the immediate task at hand. The permanence of and basis for membership in a particular context, the differential status accorded different contexts by the student, teacher, and other students, and the tasks of the context are just some of the factors that contribute to the complexity of the phenomenon known as classroom grouping. The contexts of school literacy are complex entities, influencing what students learn, how they learn it, and their perceptions of themselves as readers and writers. Creating literacy contexts that foster high levels of literacy in all students is a task that has challenged generations of teachers.

As is often the case with complex problems, a typical response to the question of classroom grouping has been to provide relatively simple solutions. A solution that emanated from the same behaviorist perspective that guided the development of norm-referenced tests of silent reading was the division of classrooms into three groups (Smith, 1934/1965). Ability in a domain such as reading was seen to be normally distributed in a population and, by dividing children into three groups according to this ability, teachers could provide materials and instruction that would be attuned to these ability levels. Several reviews that were conducted separately but published within a year of one another (Allington, 1983; Cazden, 1985; Hiebert, 1983) discussed the consequences of these small group experiences for students at different ability levels, especially for the students who struggle most with literacy. The ability status of students influenced their experiences in the group but went beyond group experiences alone. For example, children's assignments and teachers' interactions with students in literacy events beyond the small groups were influenced by ability-group status. These reviews emphasized the problems that arose when ability grouping became the primary literacy context in classrooms and when ability-group status pervaded every aspect of the literacy program—even beyond into aspects like classroom assignment.

Solutions that are complex and long-term in nature are often difficult to accept. Not surprisingly, many responded to these reviews by declaring ability grouping—and even teacher-led small-group instruction of any kind—to be "wrong" and began seeking a substitute organizational scheme. A common research design of cognitive scientists had been to introduce students to strategies in whole-class contexts. In some districts and schools, whole-class instruction became the new panacea. Problems soon became apparent to the teachers working in these districts and schools. As first-grade teachers faced a class of twenty-five to thirty students, they began to see many who did not proceed easily in a whole-class format. Third- and fourth-grade teachers with students who could not read the designated books for those grades searched for solutions that often had others doing the reading for those students who could not read the text themselves. That is, precisely the students who needed to be involved in reading to become good readers were listening to others read.

This common response to a complex set of issues, to use Reyes's (1992) label, is that "one size fits all." Other grouping formats such as cooperative learning or the individualized formats of criterion-referenced learning systems (e.g., Beck & Mitroff, 1972) could be used to illustrate this interpretation as well. Although some contexts serve particular functions better than others, none of these contexts is "right" or "wrong" in and of itself. Problems arise when one grouping format becomes the sole or only context for literacy instruction.

The authors in this volume present a perspective that differs substantially from that of the one-size-fits-all response. Not only do they recognize the complexity of classroom contexts, they argue that a variety of classroom literacy contexts is *necessary* if students are to develop as proficient readers and writers. Literacy is a multiple-faceted process and is used in multiple contexts across life situations. Therefore, the contexts in which literacy is acquired in schools must also be varied. The authors of this volume call this perspective "flexible grouping." Because of the importance of individual experiences in the underlying model, another term that describes this view is that of "multiple literacy contexts."

The adjectives "flexible" or "multiple" should not be equated with "anything goes." The goal is not to generate many organizational schemes so that a classroom can be declared to have flexible or multiple literacy contexts. The goal is to create particular contexts for particular students so they have opportunities to become proficient in particular literacy functions. The different contexts that form the flexible-grouping arrangements of the authors in this volume emanate from a framework of literacy learning within social contexts. The aim of this chapter is to describe and apply that framework for educators. Without an understanding of *why* flexible or multiple contexts are needed, a great deal of energy can be expended creating a host of contexts without necessarily improving student learning. To develop the underlying framework and its implications, the chapter has four sections: (a) a description of the underlying framework of multiple literacy contexts; (b) a description of the functions served within four main literacy contexts— whole-class instruction, teacher-led small groups, student-led small groups and dyads, and individual work; (c) an illustration of how this framework has been applied to the literacy programs of schools where large numbers of children previously struggled with literacy; and (d) forecasts on the future of this framework.

A FRAMEWORK FOR MULTIPLE LITERACY CONTEXTS

While the underlying views are rarely stated explicitly to or by teachers, students, or parents, choices about contexts often reflect different views of literacy learning. The many changes that have occurred in literacy instruction over the past decade represent a shift in underlying perspectives of literacy and of literacy learning. The behaviorist view of literacy acquisition as the process of acquiring a set of skills in a hierarchical fashion by practicing individual components has dominated U.S. education since the beginning of the twentieth century. Over the past fifteen years, another perspective has been evident in practice and theory. The most frequent label given to this perspective by theorists is social constructivism (see Hiebert & Raphael, in press). The various practices that emanate from this perspective are typically identified as a whole language or literature-based view, although Au, Scheu, Kawakami, and Herman's (1990) term of "whole literacy" is probably more accurate. Many whole language advocates see their roots somewhat differently than social constructivists (Edelsky, 1990).

A Russian psychologist, Vygotsky (1978), described the basic premises of the social constructivist perspective, which has been elaborated on for instruction by scholars such as Moll (1991) and Wertsch (1985). Literacy learning within the social constructivist view is described in relation to the social interactions that occur between human beings. Literacy is, after all, a language system designed by human beings to communicate the knowledge and beliefs of cultures. Literacy is more than "knowing" how to decode. To be literate involves understanding the purposes and uses of literacy and the acquisition of an expanding set of strategies so that many different texts can be interpreted and used. According to the social constructivist perspective, literacy acquisition is grounded in social interactions between children (or novices) and literate members of the culture. These interactions are much more than teachers serving as transmitters of literacy, and their students receptors of this knowledge in exact form. The learning of human beings involves interpreting, translating, revising, and responding to the norms and knowledge of the culture. That is, human learning is a constructive process where the knowledge of the culture can be transformed and, in the case of the acquisition process of children, may take shape in forms and functions quite unique from those the adults of the culture recognize as literacy. Literacy is not simply reproduced in exact form from teacher to student in an event called instruction.

For novices to develop into proficient readers and writers, they participate in various processes. Different types of contexts support those processes. Vygotsky described learning as occurring on two planes: (1) the social ↔ individual and (2) the public ↔ private. Harre (1984) described the nature of learning on these planes as a space. Gavelek (1991) has depicted this space in the graphic that appears in Figure 8-1.

Children's learning occurs first in social and public contexts as they see adults and older children using literacy (the quadrant marked I). Often, children are part of these events such as lapreading at home or shared book reading in a kindergarten or preschool classroom. Other times, children watch as adults around them use literacy to shop in a grocery store, write a check, read the newspaper, or navigate a roadway. Kindergarteners watch as their teachers model the conventionalized forms of literacy as they write the morning message, read a book, or write children's names on charts. As they participate and observe, children are constructing interpretations about these events called literacy. These constructions are evident in the comments of young children, such as the statement of a four-year-old that "I can't read your things [the investigator's books]. I can just read *Mom, Dad,* and *Stop.*" (Hiebert, 1979).

Interactions in public, social contexts lead children to participate in these processes in more private contexts. An excellent example of more private,

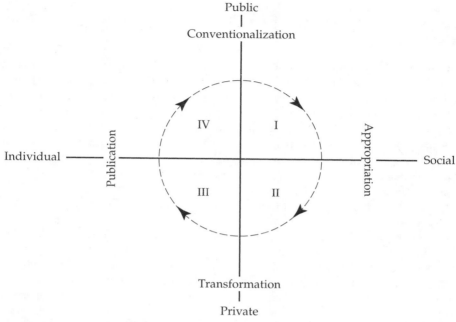

FIGURE 8-1 The Vygotsky Space

Adapted from a model by Harre (1984), from *Personal Being: A Theory for Individual Psychology* (Cambridge, MA: Harvard University Press, 1984), by J. R. Gavelek, in "A Sociocultural Perspective in Early Literacy Instruction: A Theoretical Framework," Paper presented at the National Reading Conference, Palm Springs, California, 1991. Reproduced by permission from Gavelek and from Harvard University Press.

yet social interactions (i.e., the area marked II in Figure 8-1), is provided in a videotape of Anne Hemmeter's classroom in San Antonio, Texas (Center for the Study of Reading, 1990). In a shared reading event, children chanted along the words of *Hickory Dickory Dock* as the teacher repeatedly read the nursery rhyme with them. In one segment of the videotape, two children are "reading" from the book, sweeping their hands across the page as they have seen the teacher do, although not with the one-to-one correspondence between the oral and written versions. The text states, "Hickory, dickory, dock. The mouse ran up the clock, The clock struck one, The mouse ran down. Hickory, dickory, dock." Jerry states, "Hickory, Hickory, Dock. The mouse ran up the clock. Tick Tock." Jerry's rendition may not quite be perfect but the intonation of his voice follows the cadence of reading and he is displaying an understanding that the text conveys a message. He attempts to replicate the message he has heard his teacher read from the book previously. This illustration demonstrates well the manner in which literacy modeling by adults in a social, public context is appropriated or adapted by children in a social manner, but in the more private context of the library corner.

Although the response to text that Jerry displays in the vignette from Hemmeter's classroom is movement to literacy (Sulzby, 1985), Jerry is not yet conventionally literate. Jerry will need to participate in many different contexts to transform what he has seen and heard into more conventional forms of literacy. Private, individual events (i.e., area III in Figure 8-1) such as writing responses to a book, at first with invented spelling, and pretend reading books to one's self or to a buddy illustrate the contexts in which children come to own literacy strategies.

As the responses and products of these individual or dyadic contexts are made public (the area marked IV in Figure 8-1), individuals get feedback from other members of the literacy community. They come to learn about other strategies that might have been applied, other interpretations that could be made, and the responses of their peers to the same text. Interactions where the individual's private constructions are made public relative to the constructions of the larger community lead to conventionalization; i.e., the literacy use of students comes to take on the forms and functions of the larger community. The term "conventionalization" does not mean that the constructions of each literacy user fits a cookie-cutter mold. Individuals bring unique interpretations and responses that transform the understandings of the larger community as well. What the term "conventionalization" does mean is that constructions take forms and functions other members of the community can come to understand. A student writes a poem no one has written before, but the text is no longer a series of scribbles even the author can't reconstruct. The contents of a picture book can be interpreted uniquely by a student, but the interpretation draws on the words of the author, not just the illustrations.

This cycle of processes occurs over and over again through a multiplicity of contexts experienced over time. Students do not move through the cycle in one fell swoop to become literate ever-after. The cycle continues to occur for adult readers and writers as they grow in their interpretations of a domain. For example, this chapter began twenty years ago when I was told as a beginning teacher to put my second graders into ability groups. I received unsatisfactory answers when I asked my colleagues why there had to be a group of low readers or "the pokey turtles" (the official name of the low reading group in one classroom I observed). Later, as a graduate student, I studied the conclusions of research studies and queried teachers and teacher educators about ability grouping. Finally, I wrote an article summarizing my interpretations of the literature (Hiebert, 1983). People responded to that article in writing (see, e.g., Barr, Chapter 1) and in dialogue. I began studying a new generation of organizational schemes such as reader's and writer's workshops (Fisher & Hiebert, 1990). Now I am making public my conclusions once again with the hope that this chapter will engage teachers and teacher educators to move away from the one-size-fits-all perspective of classroom contexts.

A framework of literacy learning, then, underlies the perspective of flexible or multiple literacy contexts developed in this volume. The purpose of classroom literacy contexts is to facilitate particular aspects or functions of literacy. No one context is sufficient to develop proficient readers and writers. Teacher-led small or large groups have a function different from peer-led or individual contexts. The various contexts, when orchestrated as part of a literacy program, support the creation of "whole" literacy users.

FOUR LITERACY CONTEXTS AND THEIR FUNCTIONS

In Chapter 2, Radencich, McKay, and Paratore present a set of literacy contexts (see Chapter 2, Figure 2-1). These may have variations such as cross-age grouping within a classroom or within a pair of students working together. The four contexts, however, represent the primary configurations of students and adults in classrooms: whole class; teacher-led small groups; student-led small groups, pairs, or dyads; and individuals. Before elaborating on the functions of each context, the rationale for the developmental component of the discussion about them is explained.

Inclusion of a Developmental Dimension for the Functions

Anyone who interacts with young children comes to respect the sophisticated processing in which they engage. Anyone who interacts with children also recognizes that capabilities to process text increase substantially over the elementary grades. While first graders understand Dr. Seuss's message through the voice of the lorax as their teacher reads aloud *The Lorax,* most fifth graders can read the book easily themselves. They can write an article for their school newspaper that uses the lorax's voice as a lead-in to what students can do in their own communities. Views of other writers might also be integrated into these articles as students relate their own community's efforts to those of a school described in Molly Cone's *Come Back, Salmon.*

A recognition for developmental capabilities has rarely been considered in the design of most organizational schemes. For example, ability groups were used uniformly across the grades—even though older students had the basic proficiencies that usually were the focus of the particular kind of small-group instruction associated with ability grouping (e.g., round-robin reading). When the notion of ability groups was seemingly discredited, schools that moved to other schemes such as reader's workshop again applied the schemes in a uniform fashion. First graders who relied on pictures to make sense of books spent long periods of time in independent reading, just as fourth or fifth graders did (Hiebert, Potts, Katz, & Rahm, 1989).

The differences in social capabilities of entering kindergarteners and exiting middle schoolers influence the selection and efficacy of literacy contexts. All too often, children are thrown into new organizational schemes where they do not understand the rules for interaction or the ways in which learning can be accomplished. Reports from cooperative learning are beginning to document the chaotic and ineffective learning experiences for students when guidance has not been given on the social dimensions of interaction (Meloth, 1991). A literature is beginning to demonstrate the form that guidance in the norms of student-led interactions can take, and its benefits on students' literacy (O'Flahavan, 1989; Raphael, McMahon, Goatley, Bentley, Boyd, Pardo, & Woodman, 1992).

Elaboration of Functions Best Fostered in Specific Contexts

Although most contexts can be designed to facilitate a range of proficiencies, some contexts work best for particular proficiencies. The functions described in the following discussion have been chosen to demonstrate the progression of learning from the framework (Figure 8-1), where students move from scaffolded to independent use of a strategy or type of knowledge and across public and private domains.

Whole-Class Contexts.   The whole-class context allows the strategies and dispositions of proficient literacy to be modeled, and the interpretations and information from text to be shared and extended. In kindergarten and first-grade classrooms, the teacher or other adults are the primary sources for the modeling and sharing. The beauty of events such as shared book reading (Holdaway, 1979) is that children can participate in literacy events without total skill proficiency. They can watch the hand of an adult or capable peer sweep across the page as they chant the words. Increasingly, more-capable peers model and share their strategies, dispositions, interpretations, and knowledge related to literacy and text. In the middle grades, the content of demonstrations by teachers and peers changes from foci on rhyming and story patterns to demonstrations of strategy use with more complicated forms of text and new strategies for new tasks. Rather than read-alongs of books, students engage in discussions of themes common to books or articles they have read. While first graders are eagerly chanting different parts of Mem Fox's *Hattie and the Fox,* fifth graders are arguing the merits of "the fountain of youth" as they move through Natalie Babbitt's *Tuck Everlasting.*

Perhaps the most important function of the whole-class context is the development of dispositions toward literacy. Whole-class events permit inclusion in the literate community for all students, regardless of their proficiency level at a particular point. Young children see that literacy is accessible to everyone through events such as shared reading of enlarged books. Being part of whole-class events where knowledge from text is shared, compelling issues raised in books are discussed, and the cadence and beauty of written language can be heard is a primary means for membership in a literate community. Too often in the past, the students whose entrée into the literate community occurs in the classroom have been excluded from this community in that very same classroom because they do not have the proficiencies that can only be gained through participation in a literate community.

Over the past decade, a common misinterpretation of whole-class contexts was that they were sufficient for developing the strategies, dispositions, interpretations, and information related to literacy and text. For some students who have been involved in numerous literacy events in community and home such as lapreading for young children and dinner-table conversations about newspaper articles and books for older children, whole-class contexts may be sufficient to increase their vocabulary base and the strategies that are part of new tasks such as reading expository text. For many students, however, the whole-class context is a point of departure. For students to make the strategies and knowledge related to literacy their own, participation in more intimate contexts is also critical.

Teacher-Led Small Groups. Referring back to Figure 8-1, the teacher-led small group allows students to continue to receive feedback and information about strategies and knowledge related to text and literacy. The teacher's leadership in tailoring interactions and tasks for students means that students are taking over the strategies and tasks themselves. For some students, the strategies and knowledge introduced in whole-class contexts may require substantial support from teachers in these interactions. Sometimes, these events will need to be quite focused. Gradually, the teacher pulls away the scaffolds to encourage independence and ownership of strategies and literacy tasks in students.

For young children, the content of teacher-led small groups will center around unraveling the mysteries of the relationship between oral language (at which children are proficient) and written language (which they are coming to know). One of the primary means whereby this mystery can be resolved is through repeated reading of picture books (Dahl, 1979). After the first month or so of the school year, first- and second-grade teachers may find that children's awareness of the relationship between oral and written language differs enough so that it is useful to work with small groups of children who have similar understandings. Some might call this homogeneous grouping but, I will argue, it is vastly different than the ability grouping of the past. Unlike ability groups where students were viewed as varying in their basic abilities to become literate, teacher-led small groups or needs-grouping are intended to build on children's existing literacy and to move them on to higher stages. Furthermore, membership in groups is fluid; it does not limit children to particular literacy tasks or exclude them from other classroom literacy events.

Contrary to popular conceptions, most students by the end of second grade have figured out the relationship between oral and written language (Catto, 1993). What some students have not acquired—and there is evidence this group is quite substantial among U.S. fourth graders (Campbell & Kapinus, 1993)—is automaticity at reading and writing. At the middle grades, teacher-led small-group interactions may be geared to fostering this automaticity but not with the simple, predictable books used in the primary grades. Short articles on interesting topics that relate to the tasks of social studies, mathematics, and science might be used. Lessons on word-level strategies can focus on morphological patterns rather than letter-sound correspondences (Nagy, Anderson, Schommer, Scott, & Stallman, 1989). For middle-grade students, teacher-led small groups can also be devoted to fostering the strategies required to function well in student-led groups or in cross-age tutoring contexts. An integral part of the Book Club project (Raphael et al., 1991) is to teach children to be effective at sharing information, holding conversations, and identifying material from their journals appropriate for sharing within small or large groups. Teacher-led small-group meetings can also be used productively as a time to share responses and interpretations of texts, especially those where the content is sensitive or highly charged.

Student-Led Small Groups and Dyads. The type of scaffolding teachers provide cannot be expected of peers, even cross-age peers. There are exceptions to this statement such as Juel's (1994) project where cross-age tutors were young adults struggling themselves with age-appropriate literacy tasks (the tasks of university courses). However, the contexts where students interact with one another give them occasions not afforded in teacher-led interactions. Students are allowed to apply strategies, to model strategies with less capable peers, and to get feedback on interpretations and strategy use from peers.

For many first graders, reading aloud with another student in a dyad will be much more manageable than coordinating a task with four to six other students. This caution, however, does not mean teachers should never have young children participate in small groups. To deny students the opportunity to do what they are not good at is to deny them the means of becoming good at it. But it would be expected that the ratio of time spent in student-led interactions rather than teacher-led events would increase as students move through the grades. The nature of tasks also becomes more sophisticated as students move from the repeated reading of the primary grades to the use of groups as the context for book discussions. The work of Raphael and McMahon (Raphael et al., 1992) illustrates how student-led groups can be used as book clubs where the members of the club have read the same selection or a selection on a related topic, and where they meet to discuss their interpretations and questions.

Although student-led small groups and dyads have been clustered together in this discussion, the two contexts are not precisely the same. Taking responsibility for learning and sharing one's learning with others occurs in student-led small groups, but the presence of two students rather than four or five allows for more participation and leadership. For all students, whatever the age, peer dyads are important means for sharing and applying literacy knowledge and strategies. The teaching function of older students to young ones is recognized periodically (Allen, 1976), with a resurgence of this recognition occurring currently in the format of cross-age class groupings. But even without formal reorganization across a school, cross-age groups can be created and maintained on a regular basis. First graders can read with kindergarteners; fifth graders can introduce third graders to reference materials in the school library.

To reiterate the point made throughout this section, student-led small groups and dyads serve a different function than teacher-led small groups. To expect all of the functions in learning to be served by any one context will have disastrous consequences on student learning. When peer contexts dominate and teachers abrogate their role as scaffolders of information about literacy, students' learning suffers. To ignore the power of peer teaching and collaboration, however, is also to shortchange students. Without peer contexts, students miss out on interactions that allow them to own strategies and literacy events.

Individual Contexts. Reading on one's own, establishing one's responses and interpretations of what one has read, drafting a composition, and preparing what one will share with others from reading and writing are central to being literate. The tasks of school need to be legitimate or authentic opportunities to share what has been read and written or to use that reading and writing for ends other than simply practice aimed at becoming conventionally literate. The "making public" process of one's knowledge or strategies or "publication" in Figure 8-1 give initiative and meaning to students. The lack of this authenticity or meaningfulness has created a major obstacle for many students in becoming literate. The "practice" tasks of seatwork that generations of students spent hour after hour completing were viewed as meaningless busywork, even by first graders (Anderson, Brubaker, Alleman-Brooks, & Duffy, 1985).

The design of individual contexts requires a substantial amount of thought by teachers, especially for young children. While young children's attentiveness varies as a function of a host of factors such as the book, the classroom staging of the event, the particular child's literacy proficiency, and so forth, it would not be surprising to find that many young children spend their time unproductively after the first 15–20 minutes of an hourlong period of self-selected reading. This is not to say that some children will not spend the hour productively. However, the biggest problem in many classrooms where teachers have moved to devoting large segments of the literacy period to self-selection of trade books by children is the lack of a focus in literacy events (Fisher & Hiebert, 1990).

MULTIPLE CONTEXTS WITHIN A SCHOOLWIDE PROGRAM

A teacher-researcher colleague of mine talks about revising ideas from other teachers for the group of students with whom she is working in any particular year. The level of specificity in the descriptions of multiple literacy contexts within the chapters of this volume will allow such revision by teachers for different classroom configurations. Many descriptions can be found in addition to those described here. Among many of these examples, however, there are few that describe configurations in schools with different profiles of students. For example, Hiebert and Colt (1989) describe a series of organizational schemes in literature-based classrooms. All of these descriptions pertain to third grade with little information on how children got to that point or what needs to happen next.

The manner in which specific contexts foster particular functions across a student's school career is the focus of this section. The following description emanates from a project where the aim of the teacher-researchers was to adapt literacy contexts in Chapter 1 schools to enable more students to attain higher levels of literacy. The district where this project was initiated had moved to a whole language curriculum over the past decade as represented by a new curriculum framework and assessment system. The initiation of the project and the completion of the curriculum/assessment system was no accident. Everyone liked the opportunities provided by extensive writing, self-selected literature, and book groups encouraged by the new curriculum/assessment system. However, there was confusion about what to do with students who could not read text independently, a confusion that has been expressed by other teachers when whole language is interpreted as no explicit teaching (Hiebert et al., 1989).

The most pressing need was at the first- and second-grade levels where Chapter 1 numbers were increasing. The creation of contexts designed so that students would gain the needed fluency to participate in other literacy events was the first priority (see Hiebert, Colt, Catto, & Gury, 1992). However, other needs became apparent as the first group of students who had received the intervention went to the middle grades. The ways of sustaining their strategies and interest in literacy and guiding them in the extension and acquisition of strategies related to new tasks, especially those related to informational text, became a concern. At the same time, the need to support children during their kindergarten year in becoming aware of features of oral and written language as part of the shared reading and writing events became apparent. By the end of five years, three contexts had been initiated in the classrooms of the Chapter 1 schools. The contexts differed as a function of the tasks and needs of children at different levels in school. Although not in the chronological order of initiation, I begin with the context initiated in kindergarten, move to the context of first- and second-grade regular and Chapter 1 classrooms, and end with the contexts of third- and fourth-grade classrooms. All of the literacy contexts in these classrooms are not described, only those initiated as part of the project. The intent was not to redesign all literacy contexts, especially those with which teachers were satisfied, but rather to attend to those gaps that teachers and supervisors identified.

Kindergarten

In the three kindergarten classrooms that were part of the original effort (Gury, 1994) and the dozen or so kindergarten classrooms that joined the project the second year, particular contexts were favored by some teachers more than others. Among the original group of teachers, one used learning centers while the other two did not; another emphasized independent activities to a much greater degree than the other two. One context common across the classrooms was a whole-class activity where teachers read to students. The function not attended to systematically in kindergarten classrooms where observations had been conducted (Gury, 1994) was modeling and talk of literacy processes, especially the phonemic awareness shown to predict children's success in beginning literacy (Juel, 1991). Phonemic awareness encompasses a number of different processes that involve aural discrimination tasks related to literacy. The written equivalents are not necessarily part of the task as, for example, when children are asked to make a new word by eliminating the first sound they hear in a word such as /and/ from /hand/ or /ice/ from /nice/ (Cunningham, 1990).

The project aimed to increase children's awareness of words in books and of phonemic awareness through participation in shared book reading events. These functions, however, were not to be supported at the expense of children's involvement in real reading and writing tasks. Participation in reading books that are humorous, rhyme, and/or are rhythmical, as well as writing stories about favorite things or events, give children the incentive for acquiring the more abstract knowledge related to literacy—or what Gough and Hillinger (1980) have called "cryptoanalytic intent."

Twice weekly from October through April, kindergarten teachers conducted a shared-reading event with students in groups of seven to nine (about one-third of a class). Groups were formed so that each included the range of literacy levels in the class. The event began with an introduction and several readings of a Big Book as well as the rereading of a book from the previous session. Teachers encouraged children's talk through questions that focused on concepts, including print concepts. In the next stage children examined individual copies of the books. Children were encouraged to read these books at whatever level the children interpreted to be reading, with teachers using Sulzby's (1985) twelve levels of book reading as a basis for recognizing a range of responses to the task of reading. Word play, with an emphasis on phonemic awareness, occurred next. An aural game might ask children to delete the initial phoneme of a word ("I say mice, you say?"). After listening for and orally identifying words that rhyme with key words in the text, children write with magnetic letters and with markers on dry-erase boards. These tasks are scaffolded differently, depending on children's knowledge. For example, a phonogram might be written on the magnetic board and children asked to make a word from two or three available letters (e.g., "f" and "c" might be on the magnetic board with the phonogram "at"). Children are encouraged to ask one another for help and to read to one another. An event always ended with children "reading" a self-selected part of the text to others in the group.

The kindergarten students of the three teachers in the spring prior to the project initiation in the fall of 1992 were assessed on the same measures that students in the intervention group received. The book-reading stages of kindergarten groups differed significantly as a result of the intervention. On Sulzby's 12-point scale (1 = refusal to read; 12 = independent reading), the intervention group had an average score of 9, which means their responses involved attention to the print on the page when asked to read a book. The score of 7 for the baseline group meant that they focused on the pictures as the source for retelling the story. The most dramatic difference was on phonemic awareness where the average score of students in the intervention group was almost 8 points higher than that of students in the baseline group. The distribution of scores was even more telling. In the intervention group, 31% was in the top quintile and 5% in the bottom quintile; whereas, in the baseline group, 4% was in the top quintile and 34% in the bottom quintile.

First- and Second-Grade Chapter 1 and Classroom Instruction

There was considerable diversity in the ways first-grade teachers organized their literacy periods, although all of the teachers implemented some form of writer's workshop with children writing compositions and journal entries, and with sharing of compositions in the author's chair. Other literacy experiences included selecting books related to a theme and discussing these in small or large groups and whole-class lessons with follow-up individual tasks related to word-level strategies. One teacher met with children who read at similar levels in small groups, but this teacher was an exception since whole language philosophy in the district was interpreted to mean that teacher-led, small-group instruction of students with similar reading levels would stigmatize children and do more damage than help. While the contexts were diverse, few provided much opportunity for growth in word-level strategies. In U.S. schools, first- and second-grade classrooms are the places where children are given opportunities to become fluent at the strategies conventionally regarded as reading and writing. In most classrooms of Grade 3 and above, occasions for instruction in the knowledge or strategies related to fluency are rare, and fluency with word-level strategies is assumed as children are given increasingly more difficult literacy tasks related to informational text.

In these first- and second-grade classrooms, however, children received few of these opportunities. The uncertainty about the nature of appropriate instruction for beginning readers as schools move to a whole language philosophy is not unique to these teachers (Hiebert et al., 1989). Further, the immersion in literacy events that teachers viewed as attuned with whole language philosophy did not necessarily lead to acquisition of word-level strategies for all children. Chapter 1 teachers expressed concern at the number of children for whom teachers requested services. Middle-grade teachers worried about the numbers of children unable to perform expected tasks.

The district contemplated moving the Chapter 1 instruction into the classrooms because of the trend to do so (Allington, 1991). But, at the beginning of the project, up to one-third of the first graders were receiving Chapter 1 support in out-of-classroom settings. The aim during Year 1 of the project was to use Chapter 1 contexts for teacher-led, small-group instruction, before specifying guidance for classroom teachers or moving the Chapter 1 instruction into the classroom. The teacher-led, small groups were viewed as a facilitating context, not a limiting one, with a particular level of literacy established as the goal for moving out of the small groups. Children participated in this context for only part of their school day and were not excluded from classroom literacy events. Indeed, the increasing fluency of many children meant that they could be active in many of the classroom events they had been unable to participate in in the past.

Previously, goals for Chapter 1 had been ill-defined. Chapter 1 teachers had conducted many of the same activities as the classroom teachers with students at the primary level, such as shared reading of Big Books and writing compositions, but with little consistency in guidance related to strategies or features of literacy. Chapter 1 had also been seen as a context for activities such as making art projects related to characters in books and learning to cook—activities the teachers believed children might not be involved in at home. As the goals of Chapter 1 were focused on students' attainment of fluent reading and writing, tasks moved to reading of predictable books (at least two books per half-hour session) and extensive writing on acetate slates, magnetic boards, and in consistent but short journal entries for the students most in need.

Results of the first year of the project indicated that fourth-quintile children who were above Chapter 1 students in September, and so did not receive the Chapter 1 instruction, ended the year substantially below the Chapter 1 group. As a result, first-grade teachers in these schools began working with the fourth-quintile group consistently in their classrooms, applying the same strategies over the following year. The need for extension of these strategies in Chapter 1 and regular classrooms for second graders also became evident (Catto, 1993). There were children who had received the small-group instruction as first graders who needed additional support; there were other children who had remained in the first-grade classroom and had not received the small-group instruction who could benefit from it; and there were children who moved into the school.

In all of these efforts, the intent has been to make the small-group instruction a focused and goal-directed event. These groups were not created for indefinite periods, and membership was not established by ambiguous measures or expectations. Based on quarterly assessments of students' reading and writing, children were moved in or out of Chapter 1. Further, these strategies have not been sustained with third-grade students. If students have not been successful through first and second grade, these instructional strategies need to be supplemented or changed dramatically. There is, of course, a sizable group of children in these Chapter 1 schools who transfer into third grade without a solid foundation, but the solution to that scenario is reported on elsewhere (Hiebert, Smith, & Donahue, 1994). As a result of these efforts, the number of children who have become fluent, eager readers by the end of second grade, however, is substantial. Of the children in the first cohort—those slated to graduate from high school in 2002—87% were reading at third-grade level or higher at the end of second grade.

Third- and Fourth-Grade Classrooms

With almost 90% of the children who had made up the lowest 30–40% of the school populations reading well, the question became one of sustaining and extending children's literacy proficiencies. The whole-class instruction that has been discussed frequently in recent years was the focus at this level. Ensuring the consistency and effectiveness of individual reading and writing was also of interest. Two large-group activities were initiated in the classrooms. The first involved lessons aimed at developing strategies for reading informational text. Since the strategies for facilitating metacognition or awareness of the critical features of text, especially expository text, are many (Pressley, Goodchild, Fleet, Zajchowski, & Evans, 1989) and can become confusing to teachers and students, teachers were encouraged to pick one or two strategies and to use these consistently with their students across content area reading. One of these strategies was highlighting the critical concepts or vocabulary in texts. When photocopies of the text were not available, Post-It notes were used to mark important points. A second strategy was for students to write short summaries of the text. The teachers frequently chose to combine strategies with students, first highlighting the text and then writing summaries based on their highlighted passages.

The second large-group activity was to increase the reading of short informational passages. Many whole-class activities involve the reading of entire books. When a significant percentage of children cannot read the book, teachers are confronted with the difficulties of what to do with this group. While the sharing of a book or a set of books related to a topic is an important part of the middle-grade literacy curriculum, the interest in this part of the project was to increase children's automaticity. Evidence is increasing that the reading of many middle-grade children is just not automatic enough to ensure meaning making of grade level texts (Campbell & Kapinus, 1993). Giving children passages that were short but interesting was viewed as a way of developing a shared body of knowledge in a classroom that students and teacher could discuss, and which could simultaneously support the development of automaticity.

Activities for individual contexts were also encouraged. The merits of 15 minutes of independent reading in classroom environments, and extending this reading to home, have been demonstrated (Anderson, Wilson, & Fielding, 1988). Consequently, opportunities were consistently provided for students to read at least 15 minutes daily from self-selected materials. Further, routines were put in place in classrooms to facilitate home reading and sharing.

The third-grade teachers in one school agreed to initiate this model; the third-grade teachers in another school where the children had been part of the first- and second-grade small-group instruction chose not to participate. The reading performance of children in the schools where Chapter 1 teachers had decided not to participate originally was also assessed. There were, then, three groups: (a) sustained intervention, (b) primary-grade intervention only, and (c) regular Chapter 1 instruction only. The differences between the three groups were substantial. Those students in the sustained-intervention group were reading text at an average level of 4.5 at the end of third grade; those in the primary-grade intervention only were reading at an average of 3.4; and those in the regular Chapter 1 instruction were reading at 2.6. These differences were apparent on standardized test scores as well.

In sum, then, the types of contexts initiated and emphasized differed as a function of the tasks that confronted children at different developmental levels. The additional kindergarten context was a teacher-led, small-group experience where children of a range of literacy levels interacted with the teacher and with one another. The interaction focused on guiding children in hearing rhyming words and in focusing their attention on particular words in the Big Books used for shared reading. These events occurred consistently across the school year but did not dominate other literacy events.

The first- and second-grade context involved the redesign of Chapter 1 instruction and the addition of teacher-led, small-group instruction in the classroom for those children who needed support in becoming fluent. All children continued to participate in the classroom's whole-class literacy events, self-selected reading and writing, and small groups formed around theme books. Further, when children had achieved the goal of the teacher-led, small groups, other children became members of the group. The groups were task-specific, with members changing as students' literacy needs changed.

In the middle grades, ways to ensure students' extension of strategies and development of automaticity with new literacy tasks, especially those related to informational text, became the focus. This phase of the project involved the redesign of existing contexts rather than the addition of new ones, as whole-class events emphasized strategies related to informational texts and as the number of individual and cooperative events that involved reading and writing of informational text were increased. As in all phases of this project, the emphasis was on attending to functions of literacy instruction and participation at different levels, rather than mandating that particular literacy contexts be implemented across the board in schools, regardless of their profile or the developmental needs of children. This description illustrates an important aspect of multiple literacy contexts: The contexts of emphasis may well be different across schools and across grades within schools.

MULTIPLE LITERACY CONTEXTS IN CLASSROOMS: FORECASTS

If we look ahead to a decade from now—2005—what forecasts can we make for the notion of multiple literacy contexts that has been described in this volume? How widespread will the notion of multiple literacy contexts get? More importantly, where this view takes hold, what will the impact be on students' literacy levels? These two issues—extensiveness of the practice and its support for high levels of literacy—have often been treated separately in the past. For example, ability grouping continued for decades as the sole context for school reading experiences without anyone questioning its impact on students' literacy. Many practices mushroom without substantive evidence. As staff development leaders and teacher educators work to implement a new set of practices, a commensurate amount of attention needs to be paid to the influence of these practices on students' literacy learning.

Since the concept of multiple literacy contexts is not a simplistic solution, it is unlikely it will enjoy the quick turn-around time that quick-fix solutions often have. Routines can be developed and these may be implemented on a more wide-scale fashion than is presently the case. However, even these routines will be complicated and unlikely to become quickly accepted and popularized. More models are needed, especially in relation to different school profiles and as solutions for schoolwide issues.

First, models need *to describe adaptations for schools with different profiles.* Are all of the children who require support receiving it? For example, in implementations of Reading Recovery (Pinnell, 1989), the design and role of the project has not been differentiated as a function of school profiles. Presumably, a Reading Recovery program implemented in a wealthy, suburban district will have a very different impact on a school system than a Reading Recovery program implemented in a poor, urban district. The capabilities of children are not the issue. The children in both contexts are capable of becoming highly literate. However, children's prior experiences with literacy will undoubtedly differ substantially as will the resources of the school district as Kozol (1991) has so poignantly illustrated.

The example above demonstrates the need to attend to different school profiles when considering the configuration and impact of early interventions. The models that teacher-researcher groups share with groups of teachers around the country also need to attend to the differentiation of contexts across school grades. Attending only to the early levels leaves unanswered questions about the configurations needed in schools with varying profiles to sustain the effects of early interventions and to develop strategies and fluency with new tasks. The tasks that stymie school children in the United States involve expository text but the problem is even more basic than that for many students (Chall, Jacobs, & Baldwin, 1990). In an examination of fourth-grade students' oral readings of a narrative passage as part of the 1992 NAEP (Campbell & Kapinus, 1993), a large percentage of the children in that sample, 44%, simply read too slowly to keep in memory the meaning of the text. Most of these students were able to figure out the words, eventually, but the task was so tedious they couldn't comprehend the text. Models of multiple literacy contexts need to take into account the manner in which these contexts are created and adjusted for different grades and school profiles. Finally, these descriptions of multiple literacy contexts need *to provide information on students' literacy accomplishments.* The failure of many students to become literate in a particular configuration of classroom literacy contexts should be cause for teacher-researchers, both at public schools and universities, to revisit their designs and models. Some classrooms may provide excellent contexts for student writing (Fisher & Hiebert, 1990) but may fail to give students experiences that generate independent use of conventional literacy (Hiebert et al., 1989). Other classrooms may provide students with a solid foundation of fluency but fail to interest them in reading outside of school. Strengths and weaknesses in literacy profiles of students will become apparent as teacher-researchers study a range of measures that capture the diversity and complexity of literacy. Equipped with this information, groups of teacher-researchers need to revisit their designs and revise, eliminate, and add different contexts. The contexts of classroom literacy, just as literacy itself, need to be growing entities.

REFERENCES

Allen, V. L. (Ed.). (1976). *Children as teachers: Theory and research on tutoring.* New York: Academic Press.

Allington, R. L. (1983). The reading instruction provided readers of differing reading abilities. *The Elementary School Journal, 83,* 548–559.

Allington, R. L. (1991). Children who find learning to read difficult: School responses to diversity. In E. H. Hiebert (Ed.), *Literacy for a diverse society: Perspectives, practices, and policies* (pp. 237–252). New York: Teachers College Press.

Anderson, L. M., Brubaker, N. L., Alleman-Brooks, J., & Duffy, G. (1985). A qualitative study of seatwork in first-grade classrooms. *The Elementary School Journal, 86,* 123–140.

Anderson, R. C., Wilson, P., & Fielding, L. (1988). Growth in reading and how children spend their time outside of school. *Reading Research Quarterly, 23,* 285–303.

Au, K. H., Scheu, J. A., Kawakami, A. J., & Herman, P. A. (1990). Assessment and accountability in a whole literacy curriculum. *The Reading Teacher, 43,* 574–578.

Beck, I. L., & Mitroff, D. D. (1972). *The rationale and design of a primary grades reading system for an individualized classroom.* Pittsburgh, PA: University of Pittsburgh, Learning Research & Development Center.

Campbell, J., & Kapinus, B. (1993, December). *Special studies: The integrated reading performance record.* Paper presented at the annual meeting of the National Reading Conference, Charleston, SC.

Catto, S. (1993). *Extending an early literacy intervention to second grade: Achievement of returnees and new students.* Unpublished doctoral dissertation, University of Colorado at Boulder.

Cazden, C. B. (1985). Ability grouping and differential reading instruction: What happens and some possible whys. In J. Osborn, P. Wilson, and R. C. Anderson (Eds.), *Reading education: Foundations for a literate America.* Boston: D.C. Heath.

Center for the Study of Reading. (1990). *Teaching reading: Strategies from successful classrooms* [A 6-part national teacher training video series]. Urbana-Champaign, IL: University of Illinois at Urbana-Champaign, Center for the Study of Reading.

Chall, J. S., Jacobs, V. A., & Baldwin, L. E. (1990). *The reading crisis: Why poor children fall behind.* Cambridge, MA: Harvard University Press.

Cunningham, A. E. (1990). Explicit versus implicit instruction in phonemic awareness. *Journal of Experimental Child Psychology, 50,* 429–444.

Dahl, P. R. (1979). An experimental program for teaching high-speed word recognition and comprehension skills. In J. E. Button, T. Lovitt, & T. Rowland (Eds.), *Communications research in learning disabilities and mental retardation* (pp. 33–65). Baltimore: University Park Press.

Edelsky, C. (1990). Whose agenda is this anyway? A response to McKenna, Robinson, & Miller. *Educational Researcher, 19*(8), 7–11.

Fisher, C. W., & Hiebert, E. H. (1990). Characteristics of tasks in two approaches to literacy instruction. *Elementary School Journal, 91,* 3–18.

Gavelek, J. R. (1991). *A sociocultural perspective in early literacy instruction: A theoretical framework.* Paper presented at the National Reading Conference, Palm Springs, CA.

Gough, P. B., & Hillinger, M. L. (1980). Learning to read: An unnatural act. *Bulletin of the Orton Society, 30,* 179–196.

Gury, E. C. (1994). *Interactive book reading events as the context for a kindergarten intervention.* Unpublished doctoral dissertation, University of Colorado at Boulder.

Harre, R. (1984). *Personal being: A theory for individual psychology.* Cambridge, MA: Harvard University Press.

Hiebert, E. H. (1979). *The effects of experience and developmental abilities on preschool children's acquisition of reading readiness skills and concepts.* Unpublished doctoral dissertation, University of Wisconsin at Madison.

Hiebert, E. H. (1983). An examination of ability grouping for reading instruction. *Reading Research Quarterly, 18,* 231–255.

Hiebert, E. H., & Colt, J. (1989). Patterns of literature-based reading instruction. *The Reading Teacher, 43,* 14–20.

Hiebert, E. H., Colt, J. M., Catto, S., & Gury, E. (1992). Reading and writing of first-grade students in a restructured Chapter 1 program. *American Educational Research Journal, 29,* 545–572.

Hiebert, E. H., Potts, T., Katz, H., & Rahm, D. (1989, December). *Characteristics of reading and writing instruction in whole language classrooms.* Paper presented at the annual meeting of the National Reading Conference, Austin, TX.

Hiebert, E. H., & Raphael, T. E. (in press). Perspectives from educational psychology on literacy and literacy learning and their extensions to school practice. In D. E. Berliner & R. C. Calfee (Eds.), *Handbook of Educational Psychology.* New York: Macmillan.

Hiebert, E. H., Smith, J., & Donahue, J. (1994, October). *Creating and sustaining a love of literature—and the proficiency to read it.* Paper presented at the Guy Bond Reading Conference, University of Minnesota, Minneapolis, MI.

Holdaway, D. (1979). *The foundations of literacy.* New York: Ashton Scholastic.

Juel, C. (1991). Beginning reading. In R. Barr, M. Kamil, P. Mosenthal, & P. Pearson (Eds.), *Handbook of reading research* (Vol. 2, pp. 759–788). New York: Longman.

Juel, C. (1994). At-risk university students tutoring at-risk elementary school children: What factors make it effective? In E. Hiebert & B. Taylor (Eds.), *Getting reading right from the start: Effective early literacy interventions* (pp. 39–62). Boston: Allyn and Bacon.

Kozol, J. (1991). *Savage inequalities: Children in America's schools.* New York: Crown.

Meloth, M. (1991). Enhancing literacy through cooperative learning. In E. H. Hiebert (Ed.), *Literacy for a diverse society: Perspectives, practices, and policies* (pp. 172–183). New York: Teachers College Press.

Moll, L. (1991). *Vygotsky and education.* New York: Cambridge University Press.

Nagy, W. E., Anderson, R. C., Schommer, M., Scott, J. A., & Stallman, A. C. (1989). Morphological families and word recognition. *Reading Research Quarterly, 24,* 262–282.

O'Flahavan, J. (1989). *Second graders' social, intellectual, and affective development in varied group discussions about narrative texts: An explanation of participation structures.* Unpublished doctoral dissertation, University of Illinois, Urbana-Champaign.

Pinnell, G. (1989). Reading Recovery: Helping at-risk children learn to read. *Elementary School Journal, 90,* 161–184.

Pressley, M., Goodchild, F., Fleet, J., Zajchowski, R., & Evans, E. D. (1989). The challenges of classroom strategy instruction. *The Elementary School Journal, 89,* 301–342.

Raphael, T. E., McMahon, S., Goatley, V., Bentley, J. L., Boyd, F. B., Pardo, L. S., & Woodman, D. A. (1992). Research directions: Literature and discussion in the reading program. *Language Arts, 69,* 54–61.

Reyes, M. de la Luz. (1992). Challenging venerable assumptions: Literacy instruction for linguistically different students. *Harvard Educational Review, 62,* 427–446.

Smith, N. B. (1934/1965). *American reading instruction.* Newark, DE: International Reading Association.

Sulzby, E. (1985). Children's emergent reading of favorite storybooks: A developmental study. *Reading Research Quarterly, 20,* 458–481.

Vygotsky, L. (1978). *Mind in society: The development of higher psychological processes.* Cambridge, MA: Harvard University Press.

Wertsch, J. (1985). *Vygotsky and the social formation of mind.* Cambridge, MA: Harvard University Press.

CHILDREN'S BOOKS

Babbitt, N. (1975). *Tuck everlasting.* New York: Bantam-Skylark.

Cone, M. (1992). *Come back, salmon.* San Francisco: Sierra Club Books for Children.

Fox, M. (1986). *Hattie and the fox.* New York: Bradbury.

Seuss, Dr. (1971). *The lorax.* New York: Random House.

Glossary of Strategies

Author's Chair. A strategy in which a child reads his or her writing for class response from a chair set aside for this purpose.

Book Talk. An oral and sometimes informal presentation about a book to a class or a group that highlights the positive features of the book or story but does not reveal the entire plot.

Early Bird. Read-aloud of a selection to be read by the class and/or vocabulary/background work with a group of less proficient readers before the class as a whole is introduced to the selection in an attempt to prevent rather than remediate difficulties the students might encounter with the text.

Idea Map. Use of diagrams to show the overall structure of expository text (Armbruster & Anderson, 1982). Examples are cause-effect or time-sequence diagrams.

Literature Circle. An instructional plan based on use of authentic, quality literature as part or all of the reading program. Children read and discuss books together, often without direct teacher instruction. The teacher acts as facilitator, directing groups toward literature-extending activities.

"Mumble" Reading. Reading, usually by emergent or less proficient readers, where it is intended that the reading be silent but where the reader needs to hear her or himself read. The reading is heard as a mumble.

Musical Ballads. Ballads are poetic stories set to music. Students might create new words to an old melody telling something about what they have read and enjoyed.

Narrated Murals. Murals of mostly words and phrases about a topic of study. They are constructed with butcher paper across a wall. Typically, language is generated by children during a lesson. These murals may be literature-related and are kept up in the room so children can read them and refer to them often.

Radio Plays. Skits or plays written by students and relating to what they have read. Radio plays are performed with sound effects as if broadcast on a radio. Radio plays might be tape-recorded, performed behind a screen, or aired over a school's public address system.

Readers' Theater. A strategy that works well with stories in which there is much dialogue. Students are assigned characters' parts to read, either individually or in small groups. One student or group is also assigned the role of narrator. As opposed to play production, there is little use of props. Preparation includes practicing of respective parts prior to the performance.

Running Record. Recording of a student's oral reading accuracy, noting use of the three cuing systems (operationalized with the questions: Does it look right? Does it sound right? Does it make sense?) as well as the student's use of self-correction (Clay, 1979).

Shadow Plays. A lamp is placed behind a large white sheet and students act or use puppets behind the sheet to create shadows in the form of a skit about their story or book.

Status-of-the-Class. A strategy (Atwell, 1987) that begins writer's workshop in which class members relate where they are in their writing. The teacher may then use this information to conduct a mini-lesson.

Story Theater. A strategy that works well with stories in which there is much action. Selected students pantomime a story while groups of students take turns chorally reading the story. When necessary for fluency, the teacher reads along with the groups. As each group reads aloud, remaining students enjoy the pantomime. Preparation includes each group practicing their part prior to the performance.

Think-Aloud. A strategy (Davey, 1983) where readers make their thinking public during the reading, sharing predictions, questions, clarifications, fix-up strategies, comparisons between prior knowledge and information in the text, images formed from the reading, etc.

► Index

Assessment, 113–133, 137
  benchmarks, 118–120, 124–126
  checklists, 122–123, 125–126, 128, 130
  kidwatching/observation, 27–28, 55,
    57–58, 62, 76–77, 110
  portfolios, 115, 118–132
  running records, 110, 119, 131, 140
  definition, 144, 172
Author's chair, 26–27, 171

Basal readers, 16, 29–30, 44, 48, 63, 85,
  96, 108, 138–140
  history of, 3
  vs. trade books, purchasing, 51, 67
Book clubs (see Literature circles)
Book log, 121
Budgets for instructional materials, 51,
  74, 84–85, 103

Centers, 26, 33, 38, 49–50, 60–62, 100,
  109
Change process, 79, 82–111
Chapter 1 (see also Repeated readings),
  26, 32
  paraprofessionals and special
    teachers, 31, 51, 59–63, 103–107
Chelsea Public Schools, 50–59
Choral reading (see also Repeated
  readings), 26, 32
Comfort-level text (see also Predictable
  language books), 30, 45, 54, 85,
  140
Common reading selection, 42–64
Concerns with flexible grouping, 107–
  110

Cooperative learning (see Grouping,
  cooperative)
Cross-national comparisons, 3–5, 16–
  17, 19

Dade County Public Schools, 59–63, 82,
  85

Early bird instruction (see Grouping,
  early bird)
Echo reading (see also Repeated
  readings), 26, 32, 47
Environments, classroom, 107
Expectations, 55–58, 63, 101–102,
  136

Furniture arrangements, 87–88, 107

Grouping (see also Instructional
  models; Research):
  ability, 1–20, 25, 28–29, 135–136, 150,
    154–156
  affective concerns, 11–12, 18, 19, 27,
    55, 102
  after-lunch bunch, 30
  cooperative (see also Research on
    cooperative learning), 33–34, 44–
    46, 48, 51–55, 59–62, 70, 79, 87,
    100, 108–109, 136
  activities for, 26, 34, 54
  Cooperative Integrated Reading
    and Composition (CIRC), 137
  early bird, 26, 59, 104–105
  definition, 31, 171
  individual, 36–37, 47, 52, 59–60

Grouping *(Continued)*
   functions of, 36, 159–160
   interest, 29, 34, 62, 87
   matching options to curricular goals,
      26, 28, 34–36
   multi-age, 66–67, 71, 77
   multilevel (*see also* Two-tiered
      instruction), 31
   partner, 33, 35–36, 38, 44, 48, 50, 52,
      60–61, 87, 140–141
      functions of, 35, 158–159
   teacher-facilitated needs-based, 28–
      22, 45–46, 49–53, 60–61, 68, 86–
      87, 108–110, 138–140, 161–166
      functions of, 28, 157–158
   whisper club, 32
   whole class, 44, 56, 48–53, 60–61, 150
      functions of, 26–28, 56–157

Historical trends, 2–3

Instructional models (*see also* Models of
      programs for at-risk students):
   grouping, 42–65
   in-class vs. pull-out support, 51, 58,
      104
Integration of the language arts, 55, 58–
      59, 63
Intermediate grades, 9–11, 18–19, 96, 150,
      164–166

Learning disabled (*see* Students, special
      education)
Lesson plans, 63, 88–95
Literature circles, 34, 47, 49, 66–80, 171
   how-to, 69–79
   rationale, 67–69

Making Words, 48, 141
Management of groups, 37–39, 49–50, 54,
      60, 69, 71–74, 100–102, 108–110
Materials (*see* Basals; Budgets; Predict-
      able language books; Trade
      books)
Mini-lessons, 26, 29
Models of programs for at-risk students,
      134–137

Accelerated Schools, 135–136
Early Intervention in Reading, 138–
      140
FROG (Facilitating Reading for
      Optimum Growth), 142–143
Multimethod, Multilevel Instruction,
      140–142
Reading Recovery, 15, 63, 143–145
Restructured Chapter 1, 15, 145–146
Success for All, 136–138
Multicultural issues, 34
Multiple intelligences, 69–70
Multiple literacy contexts, 149–168
Mumble reading, 26, 37, 171

National Assessment of Educational
      Progress (NAEP), 134, 167

Pacing of instruction, 5, 9–10, 15, 17,
      135–136
Paraprofessionals, 97, 103–107
Parents, 102, 136
   communication with, 58, 85–87, 110,
      126
   support from, 78, 103
Peer tutoring (*see also* Grouping,
      partner), 35, 46, 51–55, 59, 87,
      100, 136
   cautions, 85, 108–109
Phonemic awareness (*see also* Making
      Words; Strategies and skills), 51,
      61, 137–141, 144, 147, 161–162
Pinellas County Schools, 43–50, 82, 85–
      90, 96, 110
Postreading, 18, 28–29, 32–33, 54
Predictable language books, 31, 37, 44,
      48, 62, 78, 84, 142–143
   follow-ups to, 31, 33, 146
Prereading, 18, 28–29, 31, 52–53
Primary grades, 14, 18, 19, 37, 45, 59–
      63, 108–110, 115–117, 132, 135,
      141
   first grade (*see also* Reading Recov-
      ery), 9–12, 30–31, 60–61, 91, 96,
      135, 138–140, 150, 163–164, 166
   kindergarten, 11, 60, 78, 91, 135, 152,
      161–162, 166

Pull-out instruction (*see* Instructional models, in-class vs. pull-out support)

Read-alouds, 26, 32, 50, 52, 61, 63, 76, 137–138
Readers' theater (*see also* Repeated readings), 26, 32–33, 172
Reading:
content area, 36, 38, 51–52, 54–55, 59–60, 63, 165
guided (*see also* Mini-lessons), 31, 44–46, 48, 78
levels, 30–31, 51, 53, 62, 68–69, 114
round-robin, 67–68
self-selected, 16, 26, 36, 43, 47–48, 54, 140–142, 165
shared book, 27, 48, 63, 78, 153, 162
Reading Recovery, 15, 63, 143–145, 167
Reading Workshop, 59, 63, 104, 123, 153–154, 156
Reciprocal teaching, 35, 59
Repeated readings, 32–33, 55, 57, 59, 63
in Japanese schools, 4
managing of, 26, 32–33, 37, 44–45, 47, 54, 61, 139, 144, 146, 162
Report cards, 84, 110
Research:
action, 111
on cooperative learning, 18, 34, 156
on repeated readings, 32

Scaffolding, 28, 55, 58, 124
Schoolbased management, 59–60
Seatwork (*see also* Centers; Reading; Writing), 16, 18, 35
Skills (*see* Strategies and skills)
Spelling, 55, 57–58, 100, 102, 139
invented, 141, 154
Staff development, 51, 96–101
demonstrations, 98–99
professional organizations, 75, 100
program reviews, 99
school contact persons, 98
study groups, 100
visitations, 97–98
Status-of-the-class, 26, 27, 172

Story theater (*see also* Repeated readings), 26, 32–33, 172
Strategies and skills, 29, 36, 43, 45–46, 48–50, 52–54, 57–58, 61–62, 68, 137, 142, 157, 165
glossary, 171–172
Students:
ESOL, 13, 33, 51, 59–63, 102
high achievers, 13, 17, 27, 29, 32, 42, 61–62, 84, 85, 108
less proficient readers (*see also* Chapter 1; Models of programs for at-risk readers), 27, 30, 32, 36, 45, 68, 77, 79, 102, 108, 134–148
in special education, 13, 31, 51, 58, 62–63, 76, 84, 103–107, 138
Success for All, 136–138

Technology:
for inservice, 98–99
lesson plan programs, 93, 95
for students, 34, 38, 63, 87
Thematic teaching, 34, 45, 54, 60, 91, 102
Think-Aloud, 172
Think-Pair-Share, 36
Trade books, 44, 46–47, 49, 51–52, 59, 63, 66–67, 69, 71, 140
vs. basal, 30, 67, 85
definition, 30
selection, 71, 74–75
Two-tiered instruction, 26, 30–31, 59

Visitors to groups, 30
Vocabulary:
meaning, 27, 31, 44, 49–50, 52–55, 57, 61, 68, 108, 140, 165
sight, 31, 48, 61
Volunteers, 31, 97, 103–104, 107
Vygotsky Space, 152–154

Whisper club, 32
Word Wall, 48
Writing, 15–16, 37, 46–47, 63, 144–146
process, 28, 35, 46, 61–62, 137, 141
response to reading, 35, 44–47, 49, 52, 54–58, 61, 66, 72, 77–78
workshop, 63, 153–154, 163

4409.